series editor
ALAN MALEY

D0247307

WRITING WITH CHILDREN

Jackie Reilly & Vanessa Reilly

OXFORD
UNIVERSITY PRESS

WALTHAM FOREST LIBRARIES

904 000 00288109

Waltham Forest Libraries

904 000 00288109	
Askews & Holts	20-Dec-2013
372.63 REI	£21.50
4143827	S

OXFORD
UNIVERSITY PRESS

Great Clarendon Street, Oxford OX2 6DP

Oxford University Press is a department of the University of Oxford.
It furthers the University's objective of excellence in research, scholarship,
and education by publishing worldwide in

Oxford New York

Auckland Cape Town Dar es Salaam Hong Kong Karachi
Kuala Lumpur Madrid Melbourne Mexico City Nairobi
New Delhi Shanghai Taipei Toronto

With offices in

Argentina Austria Brazil Chile Czech Republic France Greece
Guatemala Hungary Italy Japan Poland Portugal Singapore
South Korea Switzerland Thailand Turkey Ukraine Vietnam

OXFORD and OXFORD ENGLISH are registered trade marks of
Oxford University Press in the UK and in certain other countries

© Oxford University Press 2005

The moral rights of the author have been asserted

Database right Oxford University Press (maker)

First published 2005

2014 2013 2012

10 9 8 7 6 5 4

All rights reserved. No part of this publication may be reproduced,
stored in a retrieval system, or transmitted, in any form or by any means,
without the prior permission in writing of Oxford University Press (with
the sole exception of photocopying carried out under the conditions stated
in the paragraph headed 'Photocopying'), or as expressly permitted by law, or
under terms agreed with the appropriate reprographics rights organization.
Enquiries concerning reproduction outside the scope of the above should
be sent to the ELT Rights Department, Oxford University Press, at the
address above

You must not circulate this book in any other binding or cover
and you must impose this same condition on any acquirer

Photocopying

The Publisher grants permission for the photocopying of those pages marked
'photocopiable' according to the following conditions. Individual purchasers
may make copies for their own use or for use by classes that they teach.
School purchasers may make copies for use by staff and students, but this
permission does not extend to additional schools or branches

Under no circumstances may any part of this book be photocopied for resale

Any websites referred to in this publication are in the public domain and
their addresses are provided by Oxford University Press for information only.
Oxford University Press disclaims any responsibility for the content

ISBN: 978 0 19 437599 3

Printed in China

This book is printed on paper from certified and well-managed sources.

Acknowledgements

We would like to thank the team from Oxford University Press, who guided us through the publishing process and made many useful suggestions, especially Julia Sallabank and the series editor Alan Maley.

We would like to thank the following teachers for trying out poetry ideas with their classes: Ni Lei and children at Peng Pu Primary School, Zhabei District, Shanghai, and Vyonne Tam and the children of Ping Shek Estate Primary School (A.M.) Hong Kong.

Many thanks

– to Edith Saberton for ideas and advice.

– to Marian Bravo for both her endless support and friendship.

– and to all the teachers (and advisors) in the Centro de profesores in Alcalá de Guadaira (Concha Julián), Aracena (MªAngeles Verdejo), Huelva (MªAngeles Hernández), Jerez (Carmen Sotelino), Osuna (Rafael Martínez) and Sevilla (Marian Bravo) who over the years have tried out activities and given invaluable feedback.

Special thanks to John, Rata, and Hugh for their patience and support for all we do and particularly this latest venture.

Dedicated to the memory of Joyce Platts, an inspirational teacher and friend.

The authors and publisher are grateful to those who have given permission to reproduce the following extracts and adaptations of copyright material:

p. 26 'Kim's game' rhyme taken from *Lift the Flap Nursery Book* by Rod Campbell © 1992 Rod Campbell. Reproduced by permission of Macmillan Children's Books, London, UK.

p. 66 *Summer*, 1573 (oil on canvas). Arcimboldo, Giuseppe (1527–93, Louvre, Paris, France).

p. 85 *The Tropics* (oil on canvas). Rousseau, Henri J. F. (Le Douanier) (1844–1910), Private Collection.

p. 103 *Van Gogh's Bedroom at Arles*, 1889 (oil on canvas). Gogh, Vincent van (1853–90), Musée d'Orsay, Paris, France.

Illustrations by Maggie Brand.

Music transcribed by Peter Vecchietti and typeset by Bev Wilson.

Contents

The authors and series editor

Jackie Reilly taught English for 26 years in schools in the UK before a change of career to ELT. She has an MEd from Liverpool University and a Diploma in Advanced Studies in Education from Lancaster University. She currently works as a teacher trainer at University College Chichester and the University of Warwick. This work has involved training teachers in the Middle East, the Far East, Europe, and the UK.

Vanessa Reilly has an MA in ELT from the University of Warwick, specializing in young learners. She currently trains primary EFL teachers in Spain, where she has worked as a teacher and trainer for fifteen years. She has also worked with primary teachers from all over the world but mainly from Austria, Poland, Hong Kong, and Japan. Vanessa is the co-author of *Very Young Learners* in this series. She is also the author of several children's coursebooks, including *Zap!*, *Cool!*, *Starter*, and a pre-school course, all published by Oxford University Press.

Alan Maley worked for The British Council from 1962 to 1988, serving as English Language Officer in Yugoslavia, Ghana, Italy, France, and China, and as Regional Representative in South India (Madras). From 1988 to 1993 he was Director-General of the Bell Educational Trust, Cambridge. From 1993 to 1998 he was Senior Fellow in the Department of English Language and Literature of the National University of Singapore, and from 1998 to 2003 he was Director of the graduate programme at Assumption University, Bangkok. He is currently a freelance consultant.

His publications include *Literature* (in this series), *Beyond Words*, *Sounds Interesting*, *Sounds Intriguing*, *Words*, *Variations on a Theme*, and *Drama Techniques in Language Learning* (all with Alan Duff), *The Mind's Eye* (with Françoise Grellet and Alan Duff), *Learning to Listen* and *Poem into Poem* (with Sandra Moulding), *Short and Sweet*, and *The English Teacher's Voice*.

Foreword

There is a quantum leap between acquiring the ability to speak and understand a language and learning to read and write it. Writing is not a natural activity in the way that speaking is. Many children experience difficulty in crossing the bridge from oral competence to literacy, even in their first language. In a foreign or other language the problems are that much greater.

This book offers an approach to developing the complex set of cognitive and motor skills needed if children are to be able to write in the foreign language. The approach is carefully gradual, offering teachers a rich array of activities for developing literacy skills. These range from pre-writing activities, through letters, words, and sentences to the text level. The book recognizes that literacy is not developed overnight, and that time is a crucial ingredient: hence the gradual approach.

It is easy for children to become discouraged when learning to write (and to read). The authors are at pains to make the activities pleasurable, personalized, and meaningful, in a learning atmosphere which values the attempts the children make. The activities draw on the full range of sensory modalities, and are integrated into the overall framework of language learning.

The situations in which children are taught to read English (or any other foreign language) are clearly extremely varied, ranging from those where the children cannot yet read in their own language (and which may have a different script from English), to those where they are already fairly proficient readers in their first language, and share a Latin script. The activities in the book offer useful ideas for the full range of situations teachers are likely to meet.

The information age in which we live, if anything, reinforces the need for literacy skills. This book makes literacy a key element in the overall teaching of the foreign language from an early age. It will be an invaluable support to teachers in helping their learners 'think literacy'.

Alan Maley

Introduction

This book is for teachers who would like to motivate children to write more creatively in English. It is primarily for those who teach English as a foreign language (EFL), as a second language (ESL), or as an additional language (EAL) to primary children between the ages of three and twelve. We examine the literacy needs of learners from the initial stages before children are required to write in English, through the stages of letter-, word-, sentence-, and text-level writing, and provide ideas for writing creatively at each stage.

The book is a resource for teachers, with ideas ranging from teaching basic handwriting skills and techniques for assisting with spelling, to providing opportunities for writing stories, letters, and poems, designing and making books, and creating literate classroom displays. We hope that you and the children will like the ideas, and have fun creating and publishing writing projects.

Objectives of the book

The overall aim of this book is to help teachers to guide children through the stages of writing to become confident independent writers. We have worked with primary teachers of English throughout the world and have identified a number of main areas of concern for teachers. To try and address these concerns we have designed activities including early handwriting skills, ways to interest children in writing English, and strategies to encourage extended writing. Once children have mastered the mechanics of writing, they need opportunities to write independently and creatively using the vocabulary and structures they know. This book contains many activities which could provide supplementary material to coursebooks, or material to build into a course plan in schools where a coursebook is not used. Some of the activities may be useful in overcoming particular difficulties experienced by individual children, or provide appropriate extension work for use in class or for homework to consolidate and reinforce skills.

Children learn to write in English in a number of contexts, for example:
- children who are still learning to write in their mother tongue, which uses the Roman alphabet, and who are now learning to write in English
- children who are still learning to write in their mother tongue, which does not use the Roman alphabet, and who are now learning to write in English

– children who are already proficient in writing in their mother tongue but are now expected to learn to write the Roman alphabet
– children who are already proficient in writing in their mother tongue, which uses the Roman alphabet, but which has a more regular spelling system than English
– children whose first language is written from right to left
– children who have already learnt a certain amount of English orally, without reading or writing
– children who learn to write in English from the very beginning.

We try to provide a variety of activities which will help teachers and children in all of these situations. The activities are intended:
– to provide teachers with a bank of ideas to engage children in writing for enjoyment
– to teach children to recognize the Roman alphabet: letter shapes and names
– to teach children to write the letters
– to engage children in activities that develop hand–eye co-ordination and pencil control
– to teach letter patterns—groups of letters which are in many English words
– to encourage the idea that words can be used creatively and can be fun
– to use **guided writing** forms which can promote writing competence
– to lead children from writing short pieces to writing longer texts
– to encourage children to use language creatively
– to provide opportunities for writing for a number of different purposes
– to suggest ways of creating an audience for the children's writing activities
– to develop writing in different **genres**
– to help teachers and children have fun writing together.

There are different views on how English literacy skills should be taught, even in English-speaking countries. For young learners whose first language is not English, the main debate is at what stage to introduce reading and writing. There is wide variation as to when children start learning English, and when they start writing in English. In some countries, English is taught orally for several years before the children start writing, while in others, writing in English is taught from the beginning. There are also differing opinions on whether children should start writing in cursive (joined-up) handwriting from the beginning, or whether they should learn to form letters separately (print) first. Ministries of education often have strict national policies on such matters, so we have not entered into the debate. We hope that this book will encourage children to write, whichever situation you are teaching in.

Motivating children to write

There are a number of common misconceptions about children's writing. For example, many people believe that writing is just practising handwriting and copying exercises from a book. There is also a common view that writing in English can be mastered simply by knowing the shape and sound of each letter of the Roman alphabet. In addition, many teachers believe that children learning English are incapable of writing meaningfully and creatively until they have a wide vocabulary and are proficient writers. As Valentine (2001) notes,

> There seems to be a 'myth' that children learning English as a foreign or second language are unable to attempt composing a piece of meaningful text until they have sufficient grasp of writing 'correctly' at word and sentence level and have achieved a certain degree of fluency regarding vocabulary range and use of structures. Contrary to common belief, children in this context are capable of achieving meaningful composition, even if their language level is quite low, depending on the way the language task is structured and the nature of support they receive from the teacher.

Writing is much more than just practising handwriting and completing exercises. It is about:
– thinking of what you wish to say and trying out the language to set down in words the thoughts in your head
– expressing opinions
– describing real and imaginary worlds, the ordinary and the fantastic
– playing with sounds, experimenting with words, making up **rhymes**, and writing poetry.

Children should be given free access to a variety of tools for writing (depending on availability). These could include:
– coloured wax crayons
– coloured pencils
– pastels: similar to chalk but with an oil base
– ballpoint pens
– pencils
– felt-tip pens
– chalk
– paint.

Children should have opportunities to write on different surfaces and not only in exercise books. These could include:
– chalkboards
– shaped pieces of paper
– paper of different sizes and colours
– card
– wallpaper
– shaped books

– books made by the children themselves
– old T-shirts
– pebbles or stones
– name labels
– memo pads
– registers.

Writing can be in many different contexts or genres, for example:
– making greetings cards
– keeping diaries
– designing home-made books
– creating word banks
– making lists
– writing letters
– writing stories
– writing reports
– creating comic strips
– writing plays.

Writing also helps children to make sense of the English they use in class when they play games, act out a role-play, or listen to a story. These are good contexts for introducing the relationship between written and spoken words, for example, by showing the text of a story-book while telling the story, or by giving out written instructions for games—at a later stage, children can write their own.

Copying the letters of the alphabet can be boring for chidren. The best way of motivating children to write is to give them plenty of opportunities to write in a variety of contexts and to encourage them to share their writing with others. The audience is usually the class teacher, but with imagination there are many opportunities for children's writing to reach a much wider audience (see also *Creating Stories with Children* and *The Internet and Young Learners*, in this series).

The enthusiasm of the teacher is crucial to the success of any writing programme, as children need to see the teacher as a skilled writer who models the writing process by demonstrating a variety of writing skills. As this book is meant for teachers all over the world in many different situations, we encourage you to experiment with the activities and make them your own, adapting them in any way to suit the specific needs and talents of the children you teach. We hope you find some new ideas for sharing with the children, or are reminded of activities which you may not have used for a while but remember as successful in getting children to write.

How the book is organized

As no one has produced a continuum of the developmental stages of writing for children learning English as a foreign or second language, there is no theoretical model to follow at this time, and there is a tendency to rely heavily on native-speaking children's experiences and teaching methods. We make use of some useful parallels with the development of skills needed to acquire writing competence in any language.

The six chapters in this book trace the development of writing skills from before children learn to write through to writing full texts: pre-writing, emergent and letter level, word level, sentence level, text level, and writing poetry. The term 'level' indicates the layers in the structure of development, in this case specifically in writing and reading. The levels are closely related as children must learn that letters form words, that words put together make sentences, and that sentences linked together make up a text. You will need to consider your particular teaching context, and the background and cognitive levels of the children, and choose appropriate activities. For example, if they are only just developing writing in their mother tongue but are also expected to write in English, you should start at the pre-writing stage. If they are already writing in a mother tongue which uses the Roman alphabet, you may decide to proceed to word or sentence level. For children who can already write, but are using a different writing system, you may need to go back to the letter-formation stage, but as the children have already mastered skills such as holding a writing implement, and understand the function of writing, they will not need some of the basic activities which are aimed at younger learners.

1 Pre-writing level

The book begins with the **pre-writing** stage. In some books this term is used when referring to exercises prior to a writing task, such as brainstorming and gathering ideas. In this book, however, pre-writing refers to the period when the children are not expected to write in English but are developing basic skills which will be needed once they reach the **emergent** and letter-writing stage. We include activities involving matching shapes and pattern-making, which are important at this level because they enhance the ability later to differentiate between similar letter and word shapes.

Younger children need to experience many activities that develop visual skills, enhance the gross and fine motor skills (for pencil control and accuracy), develop **hand–eye co-ordination**, and strengthen the muscles of the hands. Gross motor skills control the groups of large muscles in the arms, legs, and body. They are important to writing because gross motor movement influences the control of fine motor movements for using tools such as a pen, pencil, and scissors effectively. Practising sequences of large movements such as walking, running, jumping, and skipping helps chidren to remember sequences of movement and influences small-scale movements such as pattern-making, colouring, cutting, and threading. They also develop spatial concepts such as forward and back, up and down.

Doing physical activities also has the benefit of making children move around, which they need to do in order to maintain concentration. Activities involving the whole body also use the technique of **Total Physical Response** (Asher 1993), which is based on the premise that all five senses should be engaged to learn fully. Research indicates that language learned in this way may be retained longer, as it helps children to understand the target language by acting it out.

You can do various types of craft activities to develop motor skills, including painting, drawing, cutting and sticking, using threading boards, hammering, following patterns with their fingers, creating patterns in sand, drawing shapes in the air with bright ribbons or scarves, or shaping materials such as strips of clay or **playdough** along patterns drawn by the teacher on to card. This leads to **emergent** writing, which is the earliest stage in the writing process.

2 Emergent and letter-writing levels

The emergent and letter-writing levels are in the same chapter because during this stage the children will progress from practising the patterns of letter shapes to being introduced to the Roman alphabet and writing actual letters. At this level the children learn that each letter has a shape and a name, and makes sounds. When knowledge of these three qualities is secure, it should have a positive effect on the skills of reading, writing, and spelling later. From this they will be taught to identify the initial sounds in words such as their name, and learn how to replicate sounds by writing letters. This will be useful to reinforce writing skills for all children, but is particularly important for children whose first language does not use Roman script.

The term 'emergent' encompasses both writing and reading, and generally refers to the stage when children begin to communicate and interact with others by making their first marks, before any formal instruction about letters. It reflects Vygotsky's (1978) view that the desire to make meaning through drawings and early attempts at writing is a natural step in a child's communicative development.

Visual skills are crucial at all levels of the writing process. The ability to see similarities and differences enables us to match shapes and copy patterns and letters, and to remember the appearance of words. The ability of the eyes to track and co-ordinate the movements of the body and hands, and to inform the body where and how to move, is a very important skill called **hand–eye co-ordination**. Writing, drawing, and cutting require well-developed hand–eye co-ordination.

In reality, there is no distinct point at which a child moves from one skill to the next. However, the stage when the child begins to learn specific letter shapes and their corresponding sounds is referred to as the letter level. It is at this stage that young children make the connection that the shape of the letter is the sound of the letter written down (see also pages 11–15 on **phonics** and spelling).

Although we have stressed the importance of creativity, handwriting practice is an essential component of letter-level learning. Many young children learning English are still learning to write in their own language, and it may be that practice in the English class will facilitate this process. For children who use a different script, it will be necessary to teach letter formation, and for this purpose one method of teaching handwriting is included. For children whose languages are written from right to left, the English teacher must teach left-to-right orientation. We include photocopiable sheets to assist with this.

Gradually, children should be introduced to all the letters through activities such as singing alphabet songs. Learning the sounds will help children to spell those English words where the spelling corresponds with the sounds (**grapheme–phoneme correspondence**). Strategies for dealing with words not spelt as they sound will be discussed under Word level.

3 Word level

At word level children need to practise the skills of writing and spelling words to consolidate an awareness of the structure and make-up of English words. Word games and activities such as making graphic representations of words in pictograms will have the added benefit of increasing vocabulary. However, children do not need a huge vocabulary to enjoy being creative with words.

As mentioned earlier, there are different views on how English literacy skills should be taught, even in English-speaking countries. One debate is about the virtues of **phonics** (focusing on sounds and letters first) versus **whole language** (where children learn to recognize whole word shapes in context).

We believe that children need a strong foundation of alphabetic knowledge (what the letters are, and their corresponding sounds), followed by a firm structure of both phonics and word recognition. In other words, children need one set of strategies for coping with words which can be read phonetically, and a different set of strategies for the many irregular English words which do not conform to any phonic pattern.

Phonics

Phonics allow children to break a word into parts as they read (**decoding**), and enable them to use that knowledge to put words together when they write (**encoding**). Without adequate phonic knowledge, it will be difficult for children to read and write well in English.

In the phonics approach, children learn the letter sounds (how consonants go together to create different sounds, such as *t* + *h* = *th*) and long and short vowel sounds, and are encouraged to 'sound out words' for themselves, develop 'word attack skills', and learn spelling rules such as '*magic* e' (when an *e* on the end of a word changes the sound of the vowel, for example, *mad* → *made*). There are two main approaches to the teaching of phonics. Firstly, there is **synthetic** phonics, which starts before reading has begun, with the alphabet, letter names and sounds, and letter formation. Then, there is the **analytic** approach, which is for after reading has begun. It starts with whole words and then looks at letters, **blends** (how the parts of a word go together, for example, *br-ow-n*), and **digraphs** (two letters which together make a new sound, such as *sh* or *aw*).

However, an over-reliance on phonics lets children down even with some of the earliest words they learn, for example, *the*, *she*, and *he*. There are some letters with several sounds, for example, *a* can be pronounced /ɑːm/ (*arm*), /ˈæpəl/ (*apple*), or /peɪnt/ (*paint*); and some sounds are written in several ways, such as /iː/ in *leaf*, *tree*, *be*, *piece*, *key*, *quay*, *police*, and *concrete*. There are many English words which cannot be 'sounded out' and the only way to learn them is by sight, but there are so many that to expect children to learn every word visually and commit them to memory creates an unrealistic learning load for them. It therefore makes sense to offer both phonics and word recognition, for example, through so-called **balanced instruction** (Dahl and Scharer 2000) in which phonics and **sight-reading** become an integrated methodology.

Very young children learning English may benefit from being introduced to the letters of the alphabet with plenty of practice in the sounds through games, stories, and rhymes, and to the letter shapes through pre-writing and **emergent** writing activities. Older children need reading skills very quickly and may benefit from an accelerated introduction to phonics, which should be developed simultaneously with word-recognition skills through activities such as segmenting words into **onset** and **rime** (see below), rhyming games, and writing **alliterative** sentences and poetry.

If you decide to teach phonics, it should be in a context relevant to the children. Research has shown that rote learning of English phonics, with pages of exercises and rather artificial texts designed to practise a limited number of words, is of little worth. However, phonics can become a dynamic tool when explored through meaningful activities. As letters are introduced, it is important to put them into an immediate context for the children to use in enjoyable activities, such as creating their own alphabet book or a class alphabet big book, playing matching games, and card and board games.

A child's growing knowledge of the nature of sounds, and the ability to recognize and memorize words with shared sounds, is called **phonemic awareness**. In order for children to write and read English, these skills need to be developed.

Sound and vision are both important in learning words. This chapter includes listening games and activities to make children aware of the sounds in words, particularly rhyming words (those which have the same sounds). At this stage they will become aware of English words which sound the same or similar, but which look very different, for example, *there* and *their*, *light* and *kite*. Activities and games involving the children's **auditory memory** will help children to distinguish the sounds of words, as well as develop their skills of listening and concentration, memorization, and recall of words. Many young learners of English first learn words orally through rhymes and songs, which develop both phonemic awareness and auditory memory. We also include a number of art and craft ideas to make the shapes of words easier to learn and remember, which involves **visual memory**.

It is common for children to transfer the skills from reading in their first language, if this uses Roman script, when reading or spelling in English. However, if the first language has more regular spelling, the same strategies may not work with English. It is therefore very important that the children know how to pronounce a word before they make any attempt to write it.

Onset and rime

To write and spell successfully in English it is important for children to learn that most words can be divided into **onset** and **rime** (but do not use these technical terms with the children). Onset is the beginning of a word (the letter or letters up to the vowel). Rime is the ending of the word (the vowel and all the following letters). For example, *c* (onset) and *at* (rime) make the word *cat*. This can help children to recognize words with similar patterns, and equips them with skills for using spelling patterns in their writing and reading. Words which share common phonemic patterns, such as *cat*, *hat*, *bat*, *sat*, are referred to as **word families**. Playing games with rhyming words, matching alliterative pairs of words, clapping out the **syllables** in words, and writing short poems, provide a context for learning and help children master skills at word level.

Spelling

Because of the large number of irregular spellings in English words, techniques for teaching and learning spelling are important. Strategies can be taught to help children to become aware of the patterns and rhymes in the English language. A popular method is 'Look, say, cover, write, and check', which can be varied, for example, to 'Look, say, cover, spell, write, check', and extended to 'Look, cover, remember, say, write, check, correct'. This teaches children that words have to be memorized and that they need strategies to help them to do that. (See Chapter 3 for details.)

Transferring between *sight-reading* and phonics

Once phonic knowledge is fairly secure, the children can do exercises such as changing the onset to make word strings, for example, *bat, cat, fat, hat, mat, pat, rat, sat*. Because some English sounds can be represented by a variety of letters and clusters of letters, for example, /u:/ in *blue, do, shoe, through*, and *too*, and some words have the same visual pattern but do not rhyme, for example, *brown* and *own*, children cannot rely on sounds alone, so they have to use their knowledge of letter patterns when they meet similar words. A core vocabulary of words which can be quickly recognized by sight should be built up, so that phonic knowledge and sight knowledge become transferable.

Making words easily accessible in the classroom on wall displays and in word banks encourages children in the habit of checking spellings as they work. Children can refer to them as frequently as they wish whilst writing, and this helps to familiarize them with high-frequency and key words.

The 'have-a-go' stage

Children learning English as a foreign language often experience another type of **emergent writing**. This occurs when they know how to say a word in English but have not been exposed to its written form often enough to remember the spelling. The child wants to write and so 'has a go' or guesses, using his or her knowledge of phonics and **visual memory** of similar words. Depending on their first language, they may write the word as it sounds, for example, 'eight' = *eit*, 'blue' = *blu*.

Teachers often see these attempts as mistakes, but when they observe closely, they see that the child has grasped the English word very well but cannot spell it. Often, children can write a whole sentence which is syntactically correct in English, but has a lot of spelling mistakes. Whilst it is important that children learn to write English correctly, they get disheartened when they know how to say words and yet their teacher marks them incorrect when they try to write them. We think it is unnecessary to correct every spelling mistake, nevertheless, unless teachers point out errors in their writing, children will be unaware of the problem and may never learn the correct form.

What can be done about these spelling mistakes? Children should be guided to the correct spelling of the words. It is a good idea for children who are ready to attempt spellings to keep a 'have-a-go' spelling sheet, card, or pad. When a child does not know how to spell a word, he or she makes an attempt and asks you to check it. Praise the parts which are correct and, if you think the child could correct it with a little more thought, ask him or her to try again. Remind children of similar rhyming words they know or point out where they might find the word—in a word bank or on the word wall. If the onset is correct, you might refer them to a dictionary, but there is nothing to be gained from prolonging this if the child is going to become frustrated.

This procedure allows you to monitor progress and potential problems. Is there a word which is a problem for everyone? Does an able child frequently ask for words which they should be able to spell? Is the child having problems hearing individual sounds?

4 Sentence level

Work at sentence level is concerned with setting out writing according to certain patterns. The ideas in this chapter introduce some conventions of writing, such as the order of words in a sentence, the use of capital letters and full stops, and when to use punctuation marks such as commas, question marks, and inverted commas. The children learn simple ways of joining parts of a sentence with the conjunctions *and* to add information, and *but* to make a contrast. They begin to introduce reasons with words such as *because*, for example, *I like my friend because …*

Putting words together into a sentence requires some knowledge of grammar. Grammar is the 'nuts and bolts' of a language, helping to give it structure and hold it together. However, rigorous learning of rules is counter-productive, as young children cannot grasp formal, abstract grammar. Children should be immersed in activities which practise grammar in meaningful contexts. For these reasons, we have devised activities which present relevant grammar in tasks such as writing poems, annotating drawings, making greetings cards, and writing messages to family and friends. It is helpful for children to learn patterns of words in 'chunks', the grammar of which can be analysed at a later stage, but which provide a basis for becoming aware of English word order. Just as changing onset and rime can help phonics and word recognition to become transferable, parts of sentences can be exchanged, for example:
Maria lives in a big house.
Toni lives in a small house with a big garden.
Ling Ying lives in a small flat.
Sean lives in a big flat with a balcony.

At sentence level, the children are encouraged to recognize nouns and verbs, and to use adjectives and adverbs in order to clarify and enhance their writing. All the activities are planned to be in a context which children will enjoy, for example, secret messages, short competitive games, poetry, and designing a T-shirt with a slogan.

5 Text level

By this stage, young learners will have been writing individual words and short sentences, perhaps about themselves, or writing greetings cards. An exercise such as an annotated drawing may have required a few sentences written with your guidance. Some children may have progressed to writing several sentences, which, put together, make paragraphs about things which are familiar to them in topics such as family, school, friends, or holidays.

However, children at this stage need a lot of support when creating an original piece of text. It is important to use a structured approach by working on the language needed, and showing children examples of what you are aiming for, so that they have a model of the finished product. This provides **scaffolding**, as suggested by Vygotsky's (1978) **Zone of Proximal Development** theory of child development. Teachers need to teach at a level designed to extend children's learning by building upon what they already know, and providing appropriate challenging tasks to lead children along a line of progression.

Children require clear instructions and appropriate models. **Writing frames** provide this structure, enabling you to provide guidance for their writing. They give children a model to follow and break down the areas of writing into manageable chunks. Some frames provide the beginnings of sentences, whilst others have text markers to guide the children through a sequence of writing. To assist with this, we include ideas and worksheets for the use of organizers such as story frames, story maps, and other systems for organizing writing. Used carefully, they can be a springboard for free writing.

We have adopted a **genre**-oriented approach to children's writing at text level because it provides crucial opportunities for writing in a variety of relevant contexts for different audiences, giving children real reasons for writing. Messages, memos, invitations, and greetings cards are examples of writing linking the English class with what happens in their social life outside the classroom. In this chapter, they will be encouraged to write stories and plays, to entertain, and to observe feelings and everyday life.

Some activities are preceded by preparation for writing, for example, collecting information by completing a questionnaire. Carrying out some kind of challenge which lays the ground for writing serves to clarify the language needed, and reminds children of vocabulary they know. Children can plan and prepare by talking about the topic before they commence writing. You will need to judge the amount of challenge the children need.

Putting themselves in the place of others, and imagining circumstances other than their own, are important steps in children's cognitive development. Reading and imaginative writing, especially writing stories, can help promote these skills. For more on helping children to write stories, see Andrew Wright's *Creating Stories with Children* in this series.

6   Poetry

Poetry is something that can be worked on as early as Word level. Designing pictograms and acrostics encourages children to think beyond simply learning the literal meanings of words, and to look at their special qualities. By writing to a model, for example, by choosing an emotion such as 'love', and describing it in terms of how it is perceived through the senses, children can produce some very beautiful and reflective writing.

The reasons for writing poems in the English class are:
– it pleases the children to be able to use familiar language more creatively
– children can produce a complete piece of writing in one lesson
– it enhances self-esteem
– children can write at their own level: more able children will produce more sophisticated poetry
– poetry reinforces grammar in a different context from exercises
– poetry can be used with all ages—the results will reflect their different perceptions of life
– it reinforces the use of structures and functions
– poetry transfers successfully between cultures in forms such as **haiku** and **lantern poetry**
– once they have built up a repertoire of poetry writing styles, children will be able to draw upon their skills to write more freely about their ideas and feelings.

It is important to be enthusiastic and to value children's efforts, however unsophisticated their first attempts may be. When writing class poems, try to inspire the children with examples of your own or published poems, to encourage them to see poetry as 'painting' with words. There are examples in this book, but the very best role-model for children is to see their teacher as a writer, so, please, experiment and share your poems with your children. There are more ideas, especially for older children, in *Creative Poetry Writing* in the Resource Books for Teachers series.

Evaluating children's writing

Writing is a complex process, which takes time and effort to achieve, and is difficult to master in a second or foreign language. Consequently, children can easily become discouraged. In order to keep children motivated, they need carefully graded and appropriate tasks with attainable goals. They also need positive feedback, to have their efforts praised, and to have their skills recognized. Learners quickly become demotivated if they are constantly criticised. However, praise should be genuine so that the children do not become accustomed to praise for work which they recognize as not being their best.

Evaluating children's written work can be difficult and time-consuming, but is useful to monitor the progress of individual children to help in future lesson planning, and to report back to parents and school authorities. You may be required to do formal assessment tests, and must therefore follow the guidelines. If you are free to choose, however, there are a number of options.

With young learners it is best to use assessment criteria based on whether a child has completed an activity and met the aims of the lesson. With older children, you may wish to keep a detailed skills chart which you complete after each activity or assignment. This gives a very accurate record of progress over time and shows patterns of development, for example, over the year. For more information on assessment techniques appropriate for children, see *Assessing Young Learners* in this series.

If you are required to grade children's writing, it is essential to have a set of criteria which can be applied to all children, and is seen to be equitable and fair. You need to draw up a list of weightings for different aspects of the writing process, which is appropriate to the age of the children. For younger children, or those just starting to write in the Roman alphabet, you could focus on letter/word recognition, handwriting, writing on a straight line, left-to-right orientation, and accuracy of copying. For more advanced children writing longer texts, the list could include handwriting, ideas, language, structure, grammar, sequencing, punctuation, spelling, and cohesion.

Help children to set realistic goals by encouraging them to see writing as a series of steps, and making them understand that they cannot go from a blank page to a finished product in one step. Children do not like to see mistakes in their work, yet they find the process of re-drafting tedious. It is important that texts with mistakes are not seen as failed pieces of writing but as a natural stage in the writing process.

Involve children in self-evaluation strategies and in setting personal goals. Encourage them to evaluate their work against the aims of the lesson, and to use the information to plan what they could do next. You might ask them to select what they consider to be their best piece of writing for inclusion in a portfolio.

Peer-evaluation activities can be useful and informative. Children need to be encouraged to think reflectively and comment on the work of others. However, this requires a careful introduction and sensitivity to the feelings of everyone. It could be as simple as asking their opinions, for example, *Did you like the story? Which poem do you like best?* Older children could make suggestions for improvement.

How to use this book

Level

0	Children who do not yet write in their first language or whose first language uses a different script
1	Children who have started to write in their first language
2	Children who can already write quite well in their first language, but are just starting to write in English
3	Children who are confident writers in their first language
0+/1+/2+	This is the starting level for an activity, but the activity can be used or adapted for a higher level.

Age

There is a wide range of levels of maturity and interests among primary children, and children start English at different ages around the world. Some children start as young as age three or four, while others start at ten or older. As mentioned earlier, there is also considerable variation as to when children start writing in English. Here we give a rough guide, according to our experience, of the age group an activity is suitable for, but you know your children best so do not ignore activities aimed at other age groups.

Time

This can only be a rough guide to how long an activity takes. It will vary depending on the age of the children, the class size, and whether the children are familiar with the type of activity. Only you can make the decisions over how long your children need to complete each step.

Aims

With younger children, as we aim to develop the whole child, the aims will be both developmental and linguistic. With older children, there may be attitude goals as well as linguistic ones, for example, encouraging children to empathize with a cause—conservation of the environment and the protection of endangered species—or with the audience.

Materials

This section lists what you need in order to do an activity.

Preparation

This gives you some guidance on how to prepare for an activity before the lesson.

In class

This is a step-by-step guide to how to do the activity.

Variations

Ideas on how to adapt the activity to your needs, for example, for different levels and age groups.

Follow-up

Optional extra ideas to continue working on this area.

Website

The Resource Books for Teachers website

http://www.oup.com/elt/teacher/rbt

includes extra activities and articles, downloadable worksheets, web links, and examples of children's work. You are welcome to send in your children's writing. If we publish it on the site, you and your children will receive a free book each.

1 Pre-writing level

Very young children find it difficult to cope with abstract ideas, so it is important to use concrete examples to make things 'real' with the use of resources like toys, pictures, and **realia**. It is also important not to use too many desk-bound activities using pencil and paper, but to use tactile materials for them to feel and remember letters and shapes. This chapter contains a selection of activities to develop the skills of visual observation, memorization, concentration, manual dexterity, and vocabulary building in order to provide a strong foundation for writing.

The age of children in the pre-writing stage may vary from country to country depending on the education system—some children start education at the age of three and need activities to develop gross and fine motor skills, whilst other children go to school aged six or seven and may start at letter level with letter recognition and formation activities. Older children whose first language uses a different script may also benefit from activities which help them to distinguish between different letter shapes.

Developing matching, categorizing, and observational skills

Activities requiring children to match or categorize colours, pictures, patterns, shapes, and objects exercise observation skills and develop visual memory which will help with letter and word recognition at a later stage.

1.1 Matching similar objects

LEVEL	**0+**
AGE	**3–6**
TIME	**15–20 minutes (depending on the number of objects)**
AIMS	**To help children realize that two objects are the same shape even if they are different sizes; to prepare them for later recognizing the difference between capital and lower-case letters.**
MATERIALS	A big bag of objects.

PREPARATION

Collect a variety of objects of different sizes, such as teddies, balls, or books.

IN CLASS

1 Put all the objects into a big bag and take them out one at a time saying their names: *Teddy*, *ball*, etc.

2 Encourage the children to put them into object groups, for example, all the teddies together, etc.

3 Alternatively, the children could group objects according to their colour or size.

VARIATION

Repeat the activity with shapes.

1 Cut out some squares, rectangles, triangles, circles, and ovals of different sizes from thick cardboard or plastic. Check that the children know the shapes in their mother tongue.

2 Show the children the shapes and attach them to the board, naming each one.

3 Divide the class into five groups, giving each child a shape: squares, rectangles, triangles, circles, and ovals. Point to a shape on the board. The children should wave or stand up if it is their shape. Speed up once the children are more confident to make the activity more fun.

1.2 Silhouettes

LEVEL

0+

AGE

4+

TIME

15 minutes

AIMS

To develop awareness of the shape of an object. (At a later stage this skill needs to develop into an awareness of the shapes of letters and words.)

PREPARATION

Prepare silhouettes of vocabulary you wish to revise. The silhouettes need to be of objects that have distinctive shapes, for example, fruit or pets. Draw the outline of the objects on black paper and cut them out. Attach the pictures to drinking straws so that you can hold them up.

IN CLASS

1 Hold the silhouettes against a white background one by one and encourage the children to guess what the objects are from their outline.

2 Let individual children come and choose a silhouette for the class to guess.

| **VARIATION** | An optional and fun activity is a shadow theatre. |

1 Set up a white sheet tied between the backs of two chairs. Place a lamp with the light directed at the white sheet. Sit the children so they can see the shadow when you hold the silhouette between the sheet and the lamp.

2 Ask the children to guess what the shadows are. Let individual children come out and choose a silhouette for their friends to guess.

1.3 Snap!

'Snap!' is a quick-fire card game for two players.

| **LEVEL** | 0+ |

| **AGE** | 5+ |

| **TIME** | 15 minutes |

| **AIMS** | **To practise instant recognition of the shape of an object or letter; to improve hand–eye co-ordination.** |

| **MATERIALS** | Two sets of identical picture cards (20 cards or more) for each pair of children. |

| **IN CLASS** | |

1 Show the children the cards and elicit the English words for the pictures.

2 Now, demonstrate the procedure with two children. Shuffle the set of cards and deal them out between the two. Each child puts their pile face down on the table.

3 The children take it in turns to pick up a card and show the picture. If they are not the same, they put them in a third pile. If the two cards are the same, the children say *Snap!* and name the pair before their partner does, for example, *Snap! Bananas!*

4 The child who says *Snap!* first keeps all the cards in the third pile. If a child says *Snap!* but the cards do not match, no one gets the cards and the game continues.

5 If the children get to the end and there has been no *Snap!*, they shuffle the cards and start again.

6 When one of the players has lost all their cards, the other player is the winner. You may wish to set a time limit as this game can go on for a long time. The winner is the child with the most cards when you call time.

| **VARIATION 1** | Develop this activity at Letter level by making two sets of alphabet cards. You could vary the game by mixing capitals and lower-case letter pairs. |

VARIATION 2

You can also play this game at Word level with word cards. Ask the children to match words with the same initial sound and words. Children can also match words and pictures (see 1.4, 'Board Pelmanism').

Developing observational skills and memory

1.4 Board Pelmanism

Pelmanism is a pairs game played with cards, which tests visual memory as the children try to remember where the cards are.

LEVEL

0+

AGE

4+

TIME

15 minutes

AIMS

To match two objects which are the same; memory training.

MATERIALS

Two sets of identical picture **flashcards**, something to attach the cards to the board.

PREPARATION

Choose some vocabulary you want to revise. Make two picture flashcards of each item. There are many sources of suitable cards available either to buy or to download from the Internet. Depending on the age group you may want to vary the number of items, starting with five and increasing them as the children become more confident.

IN CLASS

1 Divide the board into two equal parts, drawing a line vertically down the middle.

2 Show the children one set of flashcards and elicit the vocabulary.

3 Shuffle the cards and attach them face down, in any order, on one side of the board.

4 Repeat the procedure with the second set of cards so that the children can see that they are identical to the first set. Attach them in any order on the opposite side of the board.

5 Now number each card, for example, 1–5 on one side of the board and 6–10 on the other.

6 Divide the class into groups. Ask one of the groups to give you two numbers, one from each side of the board. Turn over the cards to see if they are a pair. Ask the children to name each object as you turn them over.

7 If a team gets a pair they win the cards and guess again. If not, another team tries.

VARIATION 1	If you prefer a less competitive version of this game, the class could play against you.
VARIATION 2	Pelmanism can be played at letter level and word level. Children can match capital letters and their lower case equivalents, pictures of objects with the same initial letters, pictures with words, or pairs of words.
FOLLOW-UP	Children can play Pelmanism in groups with playing cards. Divide the class into groups of two or four. They shuffle the cards and place them face down on the desk. They take it in turns to turn over two cards at a time. The winner is the child with the most pairs in each group. It is a good idea to give each child in the group a number to indicate the order of play in the game.

1.5 Kim's game

There are many variations of this game but the basic idea is to display a number of objects, allow the children time to look at them, and then remove one or more of the items. How many of the removed items can the children recall?

LEVEL	0+
AGE	3+
TIME	**10–15 minutes**
AIMS	**To present or recycle vocabulary; to memorize a group of objects: to notice when one or more items are missing; and to remember the position of objects.**
MATERIALS	A tray, a cover (for example, a piece of fabric or card), 5–6 objects which the children can name in English.
IN CLASS	1 Show the children the objects and elicit or teach the names of each one.
	2 Now, cover the tray and ask the children to tell you the names of the objects they can remember. Show them the tray to see if they were right.
	3 Remove one of the objects without letting the children see. Show them the tray and ask: *'What's missing?'*. Repeat this a number of times. Once the children are familiar with the activity you can take more than one object away.

Rod Campbell's *Lift-the-flap Nursery Book* has a lovely rhyme which helps you to conduct this activity in English. The nice thing about the rhyme is that, when acted out, it is obvious what the words mean. Once the children recognize the rhyme, it can be used as a marker in a lesson to show the children that they are going to play Kim's Game.

Lift the cover from the tray	*Lift up the tray cover*
And counting one, two, three,	*Point to the objects, pretending to count them*
Look at all the objects there	*Point to your eyes, then at the tray*
And remember all you see.	*Point to your head and then at your eyes*
Put the cover gently back	*Lay the cover back carefully*
And now we start the game.	*Point with your index finger to show 'Now'*
Think of all the things you saw.	*Point to your head and then at your eyes*
How many can you name?	*Count on your fingers*

VARIATION 1

This activity can be developed to include first letters and then words. Attach letter or word cards to the board, cover them with a large piece of fabric or card, and repeat the same procedure as with the tray.

VARIATION 2

Instead of removing objects, change the position of two or three of them. Ask a child to come out and place them in the original order.

VARIATION 3

Cover the tray, add some objects, and see if the children can identify the new items.

COMMENTS

It is best to use a few large objects for the very young, or, if you are teaching new language, to increase the number of items as the children become more proficient.

From gross to fine motor skills

1.6 Air drawing

The children use big arm movements to draw large shapes in the air.

LEVEL

0+

AGE

4+

TIME

5–10 minutes

AIMS

To visualize and memorize shapes; to reinforce vocabulary; to develop gross motor skills.

MATERIALS

Flashcard pictures of vocabulary items.

IN CLASS

1 Tell the children that they are going to draw a big television screen. Draw a big television in the air, encouraging the children to copy you.

2 Say: *Switch on the television*, and pretend to switch on a button.

3 Show the children a flashcard of a banana, for example, and say: *On the television we can see a banana.*

4 Tell the children to think about the object on the flashcard. Now tell them to draw a big banana on the television screen with their finger. Demonstrate the action and encourage them to copy you.

5 To make it more fun and meaningful, add other actions, for example, mime reaching for the banana and peeling and eating it.

6 Repeat the procedure, drawing other objects, such as a pizza, an apple, a sandwich (the children can pretend to eat them), a ball (they pretend to throw it), the waves in the sea (they pretend to swim).

7 At the end of the activity, they switch the 'television' off.

VARIATION

You can do air writing at letter level (see 2.6, 'Letter-shape chants').

FOLLOW-UP

To move from gross motor skills to fine motor skills the children then draw the objects with glue sticks and sprinkle them with glitter, sand, or any other material with an interesting texture. (See 2.8, 'Lemon letters', and 2.9, 'Feely letters'.)

1.7 Following a pattern

LEVEL

0+

AGE

3+

TIME

10–15 minutes

AIMS

To encourage the children to draw patterns (an essential skill at the emergent writing stage).

MATERIALS

Photocopiable Worksheet 1.7 a or b.

PREPARATION

Photocopy one of the Worksheets for the children to trace over.

IN CLASS

1 Show the children the Worksheet and show them how to start with their pencils on the dot and follow the line from left to right.

2 Give out the Worksheet and encourage the children to trace over all the lines until they have linked the person or animal on the left with what it wants to reach, for example, the baby with its mother (1.7a) or the man with his hat (1.7b).

VARIATION 1

Design your own worksheets using the patterns in Worksheets 1.7a and b.

VARIATION 2

The children use different materials: felt pens, paint, coloured chalk, etc., to make pattern pictures.

1.8   Dot-to-dot

LEVEL

0+

AGE

3+

TIME

10–15 minutes

AIMS

To trace over a line to make a picture appear; to develop hand–eye co-ordination; to enhance pencil control; to practise numbers.

MATERIALS

Paper, pencils, a black felt pen.

PREPARATION

To make a dot-to-dot picture, trace pictures with a solid shape in pencil. Now draw dots in a black felt pen at intervals along each traced outline. Rub out the pencil outline and number the dots in order. Photocopy this for the children. If you have time, you can prepare several different pictures so that the children do not all have the same.

IN CLASS

1 Show the children the dot-to-dot picture. See if anyone knows what they have to do.

2 Take a pencil and count through from dot 1, and pretend to trace over the dots.

3 Give out the dot-to-dot pictures and let the children trace over the numbers to reveal the picture.

4 Monitor the children's progress and check they are following the numbers in order.

5 Once the children have finished, hold up their worksheets and elicit the English name of the objects they have drawn.

VARIATION

Copy dot-to-dot pictures on to card and punch holes along the outline for the children to thread coloured wool through. They can do this with a large needle or by wrapping a piece of sticky tape round the end of the wool like a shoelace.

1.9   Mazes

LEVEL	0+
AGE	4+
TIME	15 minutes
AIMS	**To enhance pencil control; to enhance spatial awareness.**
MATERIALS	A copy of Worksheet 1.9 for each child, coloured pencils.

IN CLASS

1 Revise the colours of the pencils, for example, *Number one is blue, number two is green, number three is red, and number four is orange.*

2 The children use the right coloured pencil to fill in Worksheet 1.9, by tracing from the pencil through the maze to the objects in the centre. The children should colour the object in the colour they have used to go through the maze.

3 Repeat this procedure for the other three colours.

VARIATION   This is a simple maze. You could draw a more complicated example for older children.

1.10   Picture stories

LEVEL	0+
AGE	5+
TIME	**30 minutes**
AIMS	**To listen to a story and identify its key aspects; to develop the skill of sequencing with picture prompts.**

PREPARATION

1 Choose an appropriate story for your class. Divide the story into parts and make some picture cards to depict each one. The story we use here is Aesop's fable 'The Lion and the Mouse' (see Worksheet 1.10).

2 Make large pictures to tell the story with.

3 Decide whether the children will do the activity individually, in pairs, or in small groups and make enough photocopies of the story.

Example

The Lion and the Mouse

1 A small mouse finds a sleeping lion.
2 The mouse looks at the lion's big head with his big mouth, his long teeth and his long hair (mane).
3 The lion wakes up and catches the mouse.
4 'Please,' said the mouse, 'let me go. One day I'll come back and help **you**.' The lion laughs, '**You** help **me**! You are so small! I'm big and strong. **You** help **me**!' The lion laughs so much that the mouse escapes and runs away.
5 The next day, two hunters come to the jungle. They use a net to catch the lion.
6 The lion roars and roars but he cannot get free.
7 The mouse hears the lion and runs to help him. The mouse eats through the net and the lion is free.
8 The lion says to the mouse, 'Thank you, my friend. I am big and strong but you are small and clever.'

IN CLASS

1 Tell the story using the picture cards.

2 Once you have told the story, give out Worksheet 1.10, showing pictures of the scenes from the story, and let the children cut up the cards if they have not already done so.

3 Retell the story, while the children put the cards in the order of the story.

FOLLOW-UP 1	The children stick the pictures on a piece of paper in the order of the story or make a simple book.
FOLLOW-UP 2	When the children are more familiar with the story, they can retell it using the pictures as prompts.
FOLLOW-UP 3	Older children can write captions for the pictures to make a story.
COMMENTS	1 See *Storytelling with Children* by Andrew Wright in this series for more stories with photocopiable pictures.
	2 This activity helps pre-literate children understand the structure of a story before they begin to write. For similar activities which practise writing see Chapter 5.

2 Letter level

Teaching the alphabet

Mastering the formation of all 26 letters of the Roman alphabet and learning their English names and sounds is a major task for children. Requirements vary according to the expectations of different countries, local authorities, and individual schools, and you should always adhere to national or school guidelines.

Which style?

If there is a handwriting policy, it may state that children should learn capital letters first, followed by lower case, or, perhaps, that children must learn both at the same time. Some education authorities want children to learn a **cursive** script from the beginning. However, teachers who are free to choose a writing style and a method of teaching the letters may welcome the following guidelines for teaching the Roman alphabet.

Basic skills

Young children will benefit from activities designed to foster gross and fine motor skills (see the Introduction, pages 9–10, and Chapter 1). Activities such as writing with different materials, drawing, cutting, tracing, and colouring pictures will enhance manual dexterity. Older children who use other writing systems may benefit from opportunities to practise letter formation until they have learnt the shapes of the Roman letters.

Once children are confident writing individual letters, they are ready to practise the skills of relative letter size, letter and word spacing, the arrangement of writing on the page, and making the transfer to writing words and sentences.

Writing techniques

Young children need to be able to co-ordinate finger movements and control a pencil before they can be taught letters. For both young children and older children used to a different writing system, lots of practice with patterns—beginning with what is sometimes called 'taking the pencil for a walk', and progressing on to patterns which relate to letters, such as circles, curves, and lines—will help the flow of writing and encourage skills in manipulating the pencil.

As many Roman letters begin with an anti-clockwise movement, it is important to include some practice of both anti-clockwise and clockwise circles. Drawing three-directional lines will help with letters like *s* and *z*. Children who write their first language with a brush may need to get used to the feel of a pencil, and may need instruction as to the angle at which to hold the pencil to write Roman letters.

It is a good idea to use paper with line guides that show clearly where the letters should be placed (see Worksheet 2.1). Laminating these sheets makes them re-usable if used with water-based pens. These guides help to keep the writing straight, and control the size of the letters so that the writing will be uniform and neat, making it easy to read. They help children to gain confidence in placing the letters and judging the size, before they transfer to other types of paper or notebooks. If you draw the lines with a black pen, the children can place the guides under unlined paper to keep their writing straight.

Teaching the letters

Most children do not learn to write letters correctly by simply looking at them and copying. Teachers often need to describe how the letter is formed while children follow the instructions. You can make these into a chant (see 2.6, 'Letter-shape chants') which helps children to memorize the movements and enables them to write anywhere, for example, at home, where examples may not be available for them to copy.

You can describe the letter shapes using words like 'up' and 'down', 'start' and 'stop', 'round' and 'across'. Children find it easy to learn that all letters 'sit' on the middle line (darker in our example) and that letters with descenders or 'tails' must 'touch' the bottom line. Letters *q* and *p* have a 'tail' which hangs down straight, whilst *g* and *y* have a tail that goes down and curls round. Capitals must also 'sit' on the dark line but must 'touch' the top line.

Many teachers do not teach the letters in alphabetical order but introduce groups of letters formed in the same way. For example:
– letters which start with an anti-clockwise movement: *c, o, e, a, d*
– those with a down stroke, which 'sit' on the line: *i, l, f, t, k*
– *s* has a distinctive shape, which is not really like any other letter
– letters with a 'tunnel' shape, which sit on the line: *m, n, h, r, b*
– those with 'inverted tunnel' shapes, which sit on the line: *w, u, v*
– letters with a 'tail' below the line: *g, y, p, q, j*
– and finally, *x* and *z*.

Although *b* and *d* have 'tunnels', it is a good idea to teach them at different times, as children sometimes confuse these two letters, especially if their first language is written from right to left. As *d* starts with an anti-clockwise movement, it can be taught as part of this group of letters. See 2.7, 'Letters *b* and *d*, *p* and *q*', for more ideas on teaching these letters.

It is important to show the children where to begin and end each letter. Mark the starting point with a dot or a smiley face, and talk them through the letter formation to the end. If the preferred handwriting style is print, say *Stop!* at the end of the stroke. If the children need to learn to write in cursive, you could say *Flick!*, indicating that the pencil should make a link or 'tail' forming the link to the next letter (see 2.6, 'Letter-shape chants').

Finger spacing

Encourage the children to use their spare hand as a helper, for example, by holding the paper still. The index finger also makes an ideal spacer between letters and later between words. Alternatively, have the children make a card spacer by drawing round their index finger and cutting out the shape to use for spacing their writing.

Alphabetical order

Although we suggest learning letter formation in groups of similar shapes, children need to learn the order of the alphabet. The first few activities in this chapter deal with this.

It is important to make, download, or buy a set of alphabet cards. See Further Reading for websites you can download flashcards from.

Teaching the alphabet

2.1 Alphabet song

LEVEL	0+
AGE	4+
TIME	10–15 minutes
AIMS	**To teach the children the names of the letters; to make the letters more memorable by putting them to music.**
PREPARATION	Make, buy, or download some alphabet flashcards from the Internet.
IN CLASS	1 Put up the flashcards in alphabetical order where the children can see them.
	2 Now, sing one of the following songs and point to the letters as you sing.

```
ABCD     NOPQ
EFGH     RSTU
IJKLM    VWXYZ
```

(To the tune of 'The worm song'.)

Alphabet song a

Alphabet song b

ABCDEFG
HIJKLMNOP
QRS
TUV
WXY and Z
Now you know your ABC
Can you sing along with me?

(To the tune of 'Twinkle, twinkle, little star'.)

3 Repeat the song slowly and encourage the children to join in.

4 Give out the alphabet flashcards and ask the children to stand up and get into alphabetical order.

5 Tell the children to crouch down, and to jump up when they hear their letter.

6 Sing the song again and the children with flashcards jump up as you sing their letter.

COMMENTS

1 You will need to sing the song regularly for the children to remember it and learn the names of the letters. It is a good idea to repeat the song whenever you do an alphabet activity.

2 'Twinkle, twinkle, little star' is on the *Super Songs* cassette available from Oxford University Press.

2.2 Alphabet line

LEVEL

0+

AGE

All

TIME

10–15 minutes

AIMS

To recognize the names of the letters, their shapes, and their sounds; to put the letters in alphabetical order.

MATERIALS

A set of alphabet flashcards, a washing line and pegs.

PREPARATION

String up the washing line at the right height for the children to reach. Display the alphabet cards around the room.

IN CLASS

1 Sing the alphabet song from activity 2.1 slowly, and encourage the children to look round the room and point to the letters.

2 Sing the song again slowly, and indicate that individual children should go and bring the corresponding flashcards.

3 Repeat this until all the flashcards have been collected.

4 Now, sing the alphabet song again and encourage the children with flashcards to get into alphabetical order.

5 Give each child a peg, and show them how to peg the letters to the line in alphabetical order.

6 Now, ask the children to close their eyes. Remove one of the letters and see if they can tell you which one has gone. They may have to sing through the song to work it out. You could make it more difficult for older children by removing more than one letter.

VARIATION 1

If you did this activity with lower-case letters, repeat the activity with capital letters (or vice versa).

VARIATION 2

Repeat the activity with both lower case and capitals at the same time.

COMMENTS

You can keep the Alphabet Line up in your classroom as a point of reference.

2.3 Alphabet trail

LEVEL

0+

AGE

4+

TIME

10 minutes

AIMS

To revise/learn the sequence of letters in the alphabet; to practise the prepositions *on*, *in*, *under*, *behind*; to link letter sounds with their written forms.

MATERIALS

Two sets of alphabet flashcards (you could have a set of capitals and a second set of lower-case letters).

PREPARATION

Hide one set of cards around the classroom or playground. Display the other set in order on the board or washing line.

IN CLASS

1 Sing the alphabet song to revise the alphabet names (see activity 2.1).

2 Divide the class into groups.

3 Tell the children that you have hidden alphabet cards in the classroom and that they must find them and put them in the correct order.

4 Tell Group 1 that they must find *a*, *b*, and *c*, and bring them to you. Group 2 must find *d*, *e* and *f*, and so on.

5 The children place each letter under its equivalent on the board.

6 Ask *Where was* a? and encourage the children to tell you where it was, for example, *Under the table*.

VARIATION	Play as a game against the clock. Teams compete to find and sequence the alphabet in the shortest time. This can be done over several days.

2.4   It's an *a* and it says ...

LEVEL	0+
AGE	4+
TIME	10–15 minutes
AIMS	**To learn that the sounds of letters in English may be different to their names, and that some letters may have more than one sound.**
MATERIALS	Alphabet cards with pictures of words beginning with each letter.

IN CLASS

1 Sing the alphabet song to revise the names of the letters.

2 Show the children letter *A* and say: *It's an* a *but we say* /æ/: *apple*. Point to the letter and then to the apple. Encourage the children to repeat.

3 Repeat the procedure for some other letters. The order will depend on how you are teaching the letters: in alphabetical order or in groups with similar shapes. If you are doing the letters in order, it is a good idea to do only a few letters per lesson.

FOLLOW-UP	Use this procedure when doing any letter activities or games as it teaches both letter names and sounds. You could do activity 2.5 as a follow-up activity.

2.5   Phonics fun

LEVEL	1+
AGE	6+
TIME	15 minutes
AIMS	**To hear the different sounds of letters and link them to the letter names.**
MATERIALS	Alphabet flashcards and flashcards of the words from your song.

PREPARATION

1 Make, buy, or download alphabet flashcards from the Internet.

2 Decide on a letter sound or sounds (some letters have more than one) you want to practise. Now write a version of the song below using words the children know and find picture flashcards of the words.

> Letter *a*. Letter *a*.
> Where are you? Where are you?
> Here in '**apple**', '**ant**', and '**Anna**'
> '**Alphabet**' too. '**Alphabet**' too.
>
> (To the tune of 'Frère Jacques')

'Letter *a*'

IN CLASS

1 Put the picture flashcards on the board in the order they come in the song.

2 Show the children the letter flashcard and sing the song, pointing to the letter as you sing it, and then to the picture flashcards as you sing the words.

3 Repeat the song a number of times, encouraging the children to join in. If a letter has a number of different sounds, like *a*, write other verses and discuss the different sound with the children. For example:

> Letter *a*. Letter *a*.
> Where are you? Where are you?
> Here in '**cake**', '**bake**', and '**snake**'.
> '**Alligator**' too, '**alligator**' too.
>
> Letter *a*. Letter *a*.
> Where are you? Where are you?
> Here in '**crawl**', '**fall**', and '**small**'.
> '**Football**' too, '**football**' too.
>
> Letter *a*. Letter *a*.
> Where are you? Where are you?
> Here in '**car park**', '**art**', and '**aardvark**'.
> '**Party**' too, '**party**' too.

VARIATION

Once the children are confident with the song, they could make up their own version. Check that the words they are using contain the sound you want to practise. Then they sing it to the class. You can put the children's songs in a phonics song book and emphasize how important their work is by choosing to sing them from time to time.

Writing the alphabet

2.6 Letter-shape chants

LEVEL

0+

AGE

4+

TIME

20 minutes

AIMS

To write the letters of the alphabet; to learn the correct pen movements; to verbalize the correct movement.

MATERIALS

Large alphabet flashcards in the handwriting style you are using, paper or handwriting sheets. (See the Internet websites in Further Reading for references.)

PREPARATION

Decide on the letters you want to teach (4–5 per lesson is enough). Prepare chants for these letters (see below).

IN CLASS

1 Show the children a flashcard of the first letter.

2 Write the letter on the board, chanting the rhyme.

3 Tell the children to stand.

4 With your back to the class, draw the letter in the air with big arm movements whilst repeating the chant. Do this to the side so that all the children can see.

5 Encourage the children to write the letter in the air and chant with you. Repeat the letter a number of times, checking that all the children are doing it correctly.

6 Now write the letter on the board, talking through the movements.

7 Give out paper or handwriting sheets, and let the children practise the letter.

8 The children repeat the shape in their books. Encourage them to say the chant quietly as they write.

9 Repeat for other letters.

Letter-shape chants

This is only a suggested format. Make adjustments to suit your needs and handwriting style. Say the introductory line before each verse and describe how to write the letter, for example, *Start from the dot and write with me…*

Examples:

a
Start from the dot and write with me.
All the way round and—stop.
Back to the dot.
Top to bottom and—stop!

b
Start from the dot and write with me.
Top to bottom and—stop.
Back to the middle.
All the way round and—stop!

c
Start from the dot and write with me.
From the top round you go.
One, two, three.
All the way round, up and—stop!

d
Start from the dot and write with me.
From the middle, all the way round and stop.
Back to the top.
All the way down and—stop!

e
Start from the dot and write with me.
From the middle, across and back.
Over the top.
All the way round, up and—stop!

f
Start from the dot and write with me.
From the top and round it goes.
Top to bottom.
All the way down, to the middle, across and—stop!

VARIATION

If you are teaching cursive handwriting, say *Flick!* as you draw the link into the next letter.

COMMENTS

The 'top to bottom' movement is important if the children are to get into the habit of writing most letters with a down stroke. Model the writing with arm movements, standing with your back to the children so that your arm moves in the direction the children must follow.

2.7   Letters *b* and *d*, *p* and *q*

The letters *b* and *d*, and *p* and *q* sometimes cause confusion. This is because they look similar and *b*, *d*, and *p* also sound alike. These ideas may help to teach the difference.

LEVEL   0+

AGE   4+

TIME   **20 minutes**

AIMS   **To help the children to recognize the shape of the letters *b* and *d*, and *p* and *q*, and link them to their sounds; to give the children a good physical and visual picture of the letters.**

MATERIALS   Letter flashcards of *b*, *d*, *p*, and *q*.

PREPARATION   Draw letter flashcards or enlarge the ones in the illustration.

IN CLASS   1 Show the children one of the letters and draw it in the air, saying its letter-shape chant (see activity 2.6).

2 Now, show the children the flashcard and ask what the letter is looking at.

3 Display the flashcards on the wall and encourage the children to look at them whenever they need to write them, until they don't need to any more.

FOLLOW-UP 1   Do '*b*, *d* tracking'. Design a grid of 25 squares with letters of the alphabet, making sure that these letters appear frequently. Ask the children to track from left to right and circle each *b* and *d*. Repeat with *p* and *q*.

FOLLOW-UP 2   Do '*b* tracking'. Prepare lines of the letter *d* with just one *b* in the line. The children must find the letter *b*. Repeat this with other letters.

2.8 Lemon letters

LEVEL	0+
AGE	5+
TIME	20 minutes
AIMS	**To practise letter formation in an interesting way.**
MATERIALS	Some white paper, lemon juice, paintbrushes, a source of gentle heat such as a hairdryer or the sun.
PREPARATION	Make an example by writing a letter on white paper, using lemon juice and a paintbrush.
IN CLASS	1 Tell the children they are going to write letters with magic ink, which is invisible. Show them the example you made earlier and heat it to make the letter appear. Show them how to do it.
	2 Let the children write some magic letters in lemon juice on white paper, and heat the papers for the letters to appear.
VARIATION 1	Before applying heat to the paper, the children try to guess which letters their peers have written, and then they use the hairdryer to see if they have guessed correctly.
VARIATION 2	At sentence level, write a message with alternate letters or alternate words in lemon juice, and ask the children to guess what the message is. They check by applying heat to it.
VARIATION 3	Write a letter or message with a white candle on white paper. To read the message, brush a layer of thin watercolour paint over the paper. The wax writing will be easy to read.

2.9 Feely letters

LEVEL	0+
AGE	4+
TIME	40 minutes +
AIMS	**To help the children remember the shapes of letters.**
MATERIALS	Large outlines of letters, glue and brushes, materials to make textured pictures such as sand, glitter, **bubble wrap**, polystyrene packing from parcels, sawdust, tissue paper to be rolled into balls, beads, or any other materials with an interesting texture.

PREPARATION	Make large outlines of letters, as large as a piece of A4 or A3 paper.
IN CLASS	1 Divide the class into groups of three or four and give each group a letter, some glue, and one of the materials described above.
	2 The children paint glue inside the letter and fill the space with the textured materials.
	3 Once the letters are dry, cut them out. Stick a circle at the starting point and let children come out and feel around them in the direction the letter is formed when we write.

VARIATION 1	You can do this activity a few letters at a time.
VARIATION 2	At word level, do the same with the children's names or words you want to teach.
VARIATION 3	The children make letters or words out of modelling clay or **play-dough**.
FOLLOW-UP 1	You could blindfold the children in turn and let them come out and guess a letter by feeling it.
FOLLOW-UP 2	Ask the children to sort the letters into groups which are written in the same way.

2.10 Name games

LEVEL	0+
AGE	4+
TIME	5–10 minutes
AIMS	**To develop the children's knowledge of letters; to show how they can be grouped to make words; to reinforce numbers.**
PREPARATION	Make cards with the children's first names. Laminate or cover them with plastic to make them more durable.

IN CLASS

1 Attach the names to the board.

2 The children have to group their names according to the initial letters. This is easier if you write the letters at the top of the board and ask the children to attach their name cards below them.

FOLLOW-UP

1 Write the numbers 2, 3, 4, 5, 6, and so on, across the board and make columns by drawing lines vertically down the board between the numbers.

2 Show the children your name and ask them to count how many letters are in it. Ask the children in which column you should stick your name.

3 The children count the letters in their own names and stick their name cards in the correct column on the board.

VARIATION

You can do the same with vocabulary from word sets.

2.11 Alphabet big books

LEVEL

0+

AGE

4+

TIME

Ongoing project

AIMS

To enhance the learning of the alphabet; to make a class resource book with the children's own work; to write labels for pictures; to give the children a sense of purpose in reading their own book.

MATERIALS

A large scrapbook with enough pages for each letter to have a page or two (although you may decide that some letters like *x*, *y*, and *z* do not need a whole page), coloured markers, letter templates big enough to be prominent at the centre of each page, a selection of pictures from magazines, birthday cards, etc., paper for children to draw on.

PREPARATION

1 Draw or print large templates of letters onto card or gift paper. You may want to cut out a capital and a lower-case version of each letter. You could use a tactile version of the letters as in activity 2.9.

2 It is a good idea to index the pages by cutting the edge or sticking a tab on each page like an address book, as this makes finding the letters quick and easy.

IN CLASS

1 As you teach each letter, stick them in the book, in the middle of a page or two-page spread.

2 Help the children to identify things beginning with the same letter. They draw or cut out pictures and glue them on the pages. If the children can already write, they can label their pictures.

VARIATION 1

Children could make individual alphabet books using small exercise books or simple folded books. They should draw and colour the letter and add cut-out pictures or do annotated drawings. New words can be added from time to time.

VARIATION 2

Make a photo album of your class using the initial letters of their names and pictures of objects that begin with the same letters.

FOLLOW-UP

When you teach the children new words, you could ask them where the word should go in the scrap book.

Alphabet recall

2.12 Alphabet hopscotch

LEVEL

0+

AGE

5+

TIME

20 minutes

AIMS

To recall letter names; to enhance learning through physical action.

MATERIALS

Playground space, chalk to mark out the squares and letters, a beanbag or a small stone that will stay on the squares when thrown.

PREPARATION

Mark nine squares onto the playground (or the number of letters you wish to focus on). Draw one letter of the alphabet in each square. You could use a large sheet of cloth if you must play indoors but be sure to secure the cloth so that it will not move as the children hop.

IN CLASS	1 Line the children up facing the alphabet hopscotch grid.

IN CLASS

1 Line the children up facing the alphabet hopscotch grid.

2 The first child throws a beanbag on to a letter and hops to that letter.

3 As the player hops on each letter, the class chants the letter names.

4 The children must not stand in the square with the beanbag in, but must carefully pick up the beanbag, say the letter in that square, and then continue to the end of the grid, turn, and hop back to the start.

5 The next child repeats the procedure.

VARIATION 1

Add pictures of vocabulary beginning with the letters in the squares. The children must pick up the beanbag and name the object in the picture.

VARIATION 2

When a child picks up the beanbag they should say a word beginning with the letter, for example, *a* for 'apple'.

VARIATION 3

The children can give both the letter name and its sound, e.g. *It's an a and it says /æ/ for 'ant'.*

2.13 Odd one out

LEVEL

0+

AGE

6+

TIME

5 minutes

AIMS

To focus on the initial letters of words; to build vocabulary; to enhance observational skills.

MATERIALS

Objects from which to make displays.

PREPARATION

Prepare a display of toys and objects in a letter pattern, with all but one in each set starting with the same letter, for example:

apple, arm, ball, animal

ball, banana, fish, bear

cat, egg, cup, car

IN CLASS

1 Elicit the names of the items in the display.

2 Repeat the names slowly, emphasizing the initial sounds.

3 Ask the children to find the odd one out.

4 Rearrange the display, adding new items, and repeat.

FOLLOW-UP 1   Prepare worksheets for the children to work out individually (see the Internet references in Further Reading).

FOLLOW-UP 2   The children can prepare odd-one-out word sets for others to solve.

3 Word level

Children should begin by writing English words they know and can use, but they also need to develop an expanding, active vocabulary. With support, they will begin to use this creatively and with growing confidence. At first, they should write about things they know and like, so activities in this chapter are designed to appeal to children, making words fun, decorative, and memorable.

Whilst in the very early stages of exploring words with children we may not be too concerned about accuracy of spelling, as they get older they should begin to write with increasing accuracy. Some strategies, once learned, can be applied to almost all English words, so techniques for **whole word recognition** feature in this chapter and there are ideas for setting up a wide range of language-related displays, such as word banks.

If children are to become proficient writers of English, it is important to teach them to recognize letter and sound patterns in words and to show them that many words share common letter and sound patterns. They need skills like how to break words down into chunks of sound and how to put them back together again, and they must learn to sight-read words which cannot be segmented so easily. This chapter presents some techniques and activities to help them reach proficiency.

Developing word recognition skills

Onset and rime skills

Children need to be taught 'word attack' strategies so that they can 'have a go' at reading words. Many English words can be broken down into sections according to chunks of sound, a process known as **sounding out**. Recognition of words with shared sounds, which is the objective of the **onset** and **rime** activities, develops awareness of the structure of words, enabling children to apply this knowledge when attempting to read and spell new words. Thus, the children are able to **decode** a new word by comparing it with spelling patterns in words they already know. Similarly, they can use the knowledge to **encode** words when writing. (See 3.2, 'I can see something', for identifying initial sounds, 3.14, 'Word family posters', and 3.15, 'Word-forming spinners').

Reading and spelling multi-syllable words

The skills used in identifying the onset and rime in one-syllable words can be applied to multi-syllable words by breaking them down into **syllables** and treating each part as onset and rime. The children then put the syllables together to read and spell the whole word. It helps if they sound out each part of the word as they write it. Encourage them to pause between each syllable so that they can hear single sounds and **blended** sounds clearly and decide which letters they need to spell the word. (There may be more than one way to segment a word, but make sure they build the word in the same way as they should say the chunks of sound.) Visual clues from word banks or an alphabet display (see below) will help the children to identify the letters needed to replicate the sounds.

Techniques for developing sight-reading skills

Some frequently used English words, such as 'the', are impossible to sound out and are known as **sight words**, because children must learn to recognize their shape, length, and the arrangement of letters just by looking at them. Children need frequent exposure to sight words in a variety of activities before they can commit them to their **visual memory**. Teaching children techniques such as 3.3, 'Word windows/cameras', and 3.4, 'Look, say, cover, write, check', which focus on the appearance of words, gives them a skill to use whenever they meet new words, whether in class or at home.

Setting up a literate classroom

Creating a literate classroom with well-designed word banks, dictionaries (both printed and homemade), and word games to support and motivate the children when writing is helpful. However, a static display is unlikely to enhance learning and children need established routines in which they use the words on display, so that it becomes an interactive resource. Just as it is important to encourage children to be independent learners, they need to be shown how to use resources for supporting writing and spelling. (See 3.1, 'Word banks', and 3.9, 'Class monster', which collects words in two stages: words that the children know and words they have yet to learn.)

A truly literate classroom is an attractive place to learn and teach in. It is more than a range of displays and it should be as much a planned part of the learning process as any scheme of work, worksheet, or activity. The literate classroom should also be a print-rich environment, with a series of visual aids accessible to all during the teaching and learning process. Where there are word banks and word walls, printed books alongside the children's homemade books, bought and homemade dictionaries, pictures and children's work on the walls, the classroom is transformed into another resource, and children will perceive it as not just a room where they go to learn English.

Word banks are a valuable resource to store words, but need a system for accessing them, whilst word walls are for high-frequency words the children can see from their seats. Dictionaries and word banks raise children's awareness of the importance of checking for correct spelling and make it more fun. Both are at their most effective when actively used and frequently referred to during lessons. Children need routines for their use and practice in using them to make full use of the resources you make and collect.

Setting up word banks and walls

On deciding to set up word banks and walls, you should:
- ideally have both
- add words a few at a time
- use letters large enough to be seen by all
- make use of colour
- make sure the word wall can be seen by all the children
- use the most frequently used words
- make sure the word banks are positioned to allow easy access
- use a filing system so that words can be found easily, for example, in alphabetical order or by topic
- remove words the children no longer need
- change the display so that it always looks attractive
- keep the display orderly
- involve the children in making labels for displays
- display children's work, for example, pictograms.

Activities with word displays

Word displays may be used for activities such as:
- teaching the features of words, for example:
  Find me a word that:
  ... starts with b
  ...rhymes with egg
  ...ends in ight
- asking children to copy as many words as they can in one minute
- finding all the adjectives, nouns, etc.
- allocating time to read words from the display, for example, on a topic
- removing labels from the furniture and letting the children replace them (you could make it a team race against the clock)
- displaying key words from a story (and asking the children to order them in sequence)
- with older children, you may display some spelling mistakes and ask them to find them. (Remove them after the activity!)

Other features of a literate classroom

– it is a good idea to have an alphabet frieze for the children to refer to and which you can use to give support in games such as 3.2, 'I can see something'
– have a number of picture and children's dictionaries for reference, for them to look at when they have a spare moment
– label the classroom, for example, *door, board, coats, books, story corner, window*
– have picture/word card sets for them to play matching games
– if the children have made an alphabet big book or a photo alphabet book, display these where the children can look at them
– put stories you have told in class in the story corner or library for the children to look at
– put prompts for classroom language around the room to remind the children, for example, *How do you spell …? How do you say …? Can I have a/an …? Can I go to the toilet, please?*
– at text level, have reminders about sentence formation
– display lists of story starters, for example, *When I was very small … On my birthday, I got a very unusual present … At my grandmother's house …*

3.1   Word banks

LEVEL	1+
AGE	4–10
TIME	**15 minutes each session (ongoing project)**
AIMS	**To display new words; to store learned words for the children to refer to as they need them for writing; to enhance word recognition and develop sight vocabulary.**
MATERIALS	Posters, cards, something to fix the cards to the posters.

PREPARATION

1 Make 'word bank' posters for each letter of the alphabet, using words the children know. Attach a pocket to each poster to store words as they are learned, so that they are easily accessible to the children when you are revising/recycling vocabulary. Pockets can be made from card, envelopes, or brightly coloured gift bags which are both attractive and durable.

2 Prepare some word cards and blank cards.

IN CLASS

1 Show the children the posters.

2 Show them the word cards you have made and ask for volunteers to place them on the correct poster.

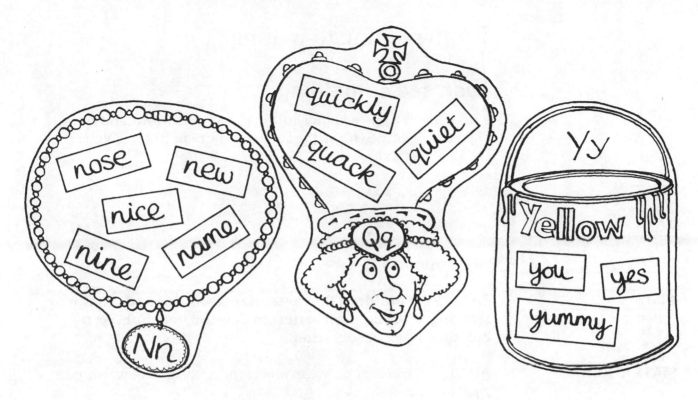

3 Elicit other words that could go on them and write them on cards.

4 The children make cards with their own pictograms and other illustrated words and place them on the correct poster.

VARIATION

As topics are also very important in the word learning process, it is helpful to make banks on topics, for example, a fridge for food vocabulary, a wardrobe for clothes, or a box for toys. The children can take words from the alphabet word banks and place them in the topic banks and vice versa. A valuable exercise is to give the children a pile of mixed word cards for them to file into topic banks.

FOLLOW-UP 1

In later lessons, remove the word cards and see if the children can put them in the correct banks.

FOLLOW-UP 2

When you work on new words, make cards to put in the banks. Move known words to the pockets.

FOLLOW-UP 3

Tell the children they can borrow the cards when they need them to check a spelling, but that they must replace them in the correct bank.

COMMENTS

1 Because the children are going to use the cards for copying when writing, it is best that the teacher should write them. They should be the best example of letter formation. Children could make pictograms and illustrate the words.

2 It is not necessary to make all the posters at once, but as they are needed, when the children have been introduced to a number of new words starting with a particular letter or a topic.

From reading to writing

3.2 I can see something

This game is 'I spy with my little eye', with the words and rules changed slightly to make the language more useful to children in the EFL context.

LEVEL	1+
AGE	4+
TIME	**20–30 minutes**
AIMS	**To help the children link letter names and sounds to words starting with the same letter; to develop vocabulary; to enhance word recognition.**
MATERIALS	Alphabet flashcards or frieze, objects or flashcards of words you wish to practise.
PREPARATION	Make a list of words you want to revise. Make sure there are enough objects or pictures in the room. If there are not enough things the children can name in English, you could 'plant' objects and flashcards around the room.

IN CLASS

1 Sing the alphabet song from activity 2.1.

2 If you have a similar game to 'I spy' in your culture, tell the children that they are going to play it in English.

3 Say, for example, *I can see something. It starts with* t *but we say* /t/. Point to the letter *t* at first to help the children.

4 You could give them extra clues such as … *and it's blue*, or … *and it's got four legs*.

5 Write the words on the board as the game progresses.

FOLLOW-UP 1

1 At the end of the game ask the children to look carefully at each word.

2 Blank out certain letters and ask children to come to the board and fill in the missing letters.

FOLLOW-UP 2

1 Use the 'Look, say, cover, write, check' method (activity 3.4) to reinforce and write each word.

2 Erase the words from the board and tell the children to close their books.

3 Put the children into groups and tell them they have three minutes to try to write as many words as they can from the game. The winning group is the one with the most words spelt correctly.

| VARIATION 1 | You could help the children by giving the final sound of the object as well as the initial one, for example, *I can see something. It starts with /b/ and ends with /k/* (book). |

| VARIATION 2 | You can choose to give the children either the sound, for example, /t/ or the letter, for example, *t*, or both, as above. |

3.3 Word windows/cameras

| LEVEL | 1+ |

| AGE | 6–12 |

| TIME | 20–30 |

| AIMS | **To concentrate on the appearance of individual words; to help children to remember how words are spelt; and to develop sight vocabulary.** |

| PREPARATION | 1 Make a word window or camera by using Worksheet 3.3 (enlarge it if you wish). Cut out the hole in the middle, making it large enough to view the words on the classroom walls, in word banks, etc. You could copy it onto card to make it more durable. |
| | 2 Make sure there are a number of words displayed on the wall or board. |

IN CLASS	1 Show the children your word window/camera.
	2 Look through the window/camera at one of the words on the wall or board and say: *I can see a word. It starts with* a *and we say* /æ/ (saying the letter and its sound). Concentrate on words you want the children to learn to write, for example, a vocabulary set such as 'food'.
	3 Ask a child to take the window/camera and try to find the word by putting the window/camera over it.
	4 Now get the class to read the word and concentrate on how it is spelt.
	5 Model writing the word on the board.
	6 Repeat this procedure a number of times.
	7 You could then get the children to copy the words to record them in their wordbook. Copying the words in different colours might make them more memorable. The children could choose different colours for different topics.

| FOLLOW-UP | 1 Make a copy of the window/camera from Worksheet 3.3 for each child in the class. Make them quite small as the children are going to look for words in their books. |

2 If you are using a coursebook, worksheet, or reader, you could say: *I can see a word. It starts with ...* (say a letter). Encourage the children to use their window/camera to frame the word. If you are concentrating on the spelling of words, you can ask the children to frame them in their books using their windows/cameras.

3 The children copy the word on some paper, then turn the paper over and try to write it from memory.

3.4 Look, say, cover, write, check

LEVEL	1+
AGE	6+
TIME	**5 minutes (or as needed when checking words)**
AIMS	**To try and fix words in the children's visual memory; to allow children to 'have a go' at writing words they have learnt; and to enhance word recognition.**
MATERIALS	A piece of card big enough to cover up a word on the board, something to attach the card to the board.
IN CLASS	

1 Write a word on the board.

2 Tell the children that you are going to give them one minute to concentrate on the word (giving a time limit makes the activity more like a game). Help the children by telling them to focus first on what the word means, then on how many letters it has, what the first and last letters are, whether the letters all sit on the line or whether there are letters with a tail, and so on.

3 Once the time is up, cover the word and ask the children to try and write it in their books.

4 Now uncover the word and get them to check whether they were right.

5 If they made mistakes, help them to see where they went wrong.

6 Repeat this a number of times with other words.

FOLLOW-UP   Encourage the children to use this method whenever they are learning new words.

3.5 Word cubes

LEVEL	1+
AGE	6+
TIME	10–20 minutes
AIMS	**To match words and pictures; to make words more memorable; to make learning vocabulary more fun; to enhance sight-reading skills.**
MATERIALS	Pencils and paper, a cube made from a box or Worksheet 3.5 (copied on to card) for each group of 4–5 children.

PREPARATION

1 Prepare the word cubes (one per group).

2 Cut out pictures of vocabulary you want to revise from magazines, for example, food, prepositions, etc.

3 Stick different pictures on each face of the cube.

4 Prepare word cards with the names of the objects in the pictures and put them inside the cubes.

IN CLASS

1 Show the children a cube. Try and elicit the names of the pictures on the different faces.

2 Now write one of the words on the board and ask for volunteers to come and point to the picture it goes with on the cube. Repeat this a number of times with different words.

3 Divide the class into groups of four or five and give each group a cube, paper, and a pencil.

4 The children open their cube, take out the words, and try to match the words to the pictures.

5 They take it in turns to throw the picture cube.

6 The children must match a word to the picture which is face up. If children do this successfully, they write the word on their paper. They can only write the same word once. You can stop the game whenever you like and the winner is the one with the most words.

VARIATION 1

If you have time, the children can make their own cubes.

VARIATION 2

Make two cubes per group, one with pictures and the other with the corresponding words. The children throw both and try to get a match.

VARIATION 3

The children can have personal spelling boxes to store words they find difficult to spell. Difficult elements of words can be highlighted in colour, for example, *two*, *eight*.

COMMENTS	1 At the start of the school year, it is a good idea to send a list of household recyclables you would like parents to save for you. For this activity, the empty boxes from face creams are very useful.

2 This is a good game for fast finishers, who can take a cube and play independently. It is also helpful for children who may need more practice with vocabulary before starting writing activities.

3.6 How many letters?

LEVEL

2+

AGE

6+

TIME

10 minutes +

AIMS

To familiarize children with the written form of words they know orally; to learn that some English words have more letters than sounds, and to learn the spelling of those words.

MATERIALS

Matching pairs of word and picture cards.

IN CLASS

1 Randomly attach the words and pictures to the board.

2 Invite children to come to the board and match the words and pictures.

3 Choose one of the words and ask the children how many letters it has and what the first/last letter is. Some languages do not pronounce the endings of words so it is important for children to realize that they must pronounce them in English. It may also help them remember the spelling.

FOLLOW-UP

You could encourage the children to sort the word cards into words with 3, 4, or 5 letters, and so on, as they did with their names in 2.10, 'Name games'.

VARIATION

1 Phoneme count activities can help to teach that some English sounds have more than one letter. To demonstrate this, write a word on the board and ask the children to count the letters.

2 Write the number of letters next to the written word, for example, *brown: 5*.

3 Next, ask them to say the sounds with you and hold up your fingers as you slowly articulate each sound: /b/ /r/ /aʊ/ /n/. Ask the children to count how many fingers you are holding up. Point to the written word and show how the two letters *b* and *r* make an **initial consonant blend**. Tell the children they need to push the sounds together. Show how the letters *o* and *w* make one sound, the diphthong /aʊ/, by holding two fingers together.

3.7 Clapping games

LEVEL	2+
AGE	6+
TIME	10–15 minutes
AIMS	**To practise pronunciation; to focus on syllables.**
MATERIALS	A list of words you want to focus on, pictures of these items.

IN CLASS

1 Write one of the words on the board. Show the children the pictures and encourage them to say *No* until you show them the picture which corresponds to the word you wrote, when they must say *Yes*.

2 Now clap the number of **syllables** in the word and encourage the children to copy you, for example, *ap-ple*: two claps.

3 Add more words to the board and clap the syllables.

4 Now play a guessing game by clapping a word and trying to elicit the answer. Accept any correct answer with the correct number of syllables. Repeat this a number of times.

5 Once the children are confident, individuals could clap words for their classmates to guess.

VARIATION 1	Clap children's names and see if the class can identify who it is.
VARIATION 2	Clap the rhythm of a word and the class must respond with the same rhythm.
VARIATION 3	Use an instrument such as a kazoo or a drum.

Making words memorable

3.8 Pictograms

LEVEL	1+
AGE	6+
TIME	15–20 minutes
AIMS	**To make words more memorable; to focus on the shape of letters and words.**

PREPARATION   Prepare some pictograms on large sheets of paper, using words the children are familiar with.

Examples: eye, snake, orange.

IN CLASS

1   Show the children your pictograms.

2   Ask: *What can you see?*, trying to elicit that the picture shows the meaning of the word. (The children may answer in their mother tongue.)

3   Ask the children if they can think of any other words they can do this with.

4   Help them to make some of their suggestions into pictograms.

5   In pairs, the children look through their coursebooks or around the classroom for more words they can make into pictograms, for example, parts of the body.

6   The children plan their pictograms in draft form, whilst you monitor and help where necessary.

7   Finally, the children draw their pictograms on a clean sheet of paper and colour it. You can display the pictures on the wall in topic groups or alphabetically, or add them to the word banks (see activity 3.1).

VARIATION 1   At sentence/text level the children could write messages or texts inserting pictograms.

Examples:

I have blue eyes

I am TALL

I like bananas

VARIATION 2   Use scrap materials to make words. Old gift-wrap could make some words instantly recognizable, for example, glittery silver paper for 'star' or glittery blue paper for 'fish'. You could also use other materials, for example, cotton wool balls to spell out 'cloud' or 'sheep', wool for 'hair'.

VARIATION 3   Make words that look like their meanings (see the illustration below). Place them in word banks or display them in the room. Ask the children to design some of their own.

VARIATION 4   If you have a computer, you and the children can type words and change the font and the colour to illustrate their meaning, for example:

pretty (You could change the colour to pink or purple.)

BIG

small

fat

FUNNY

FOLLOW-UP   You could create a Pictogram Dictionary using a large scrapbook. The children can order their words either by topic or alphabetically, adding to the book as they think of new ones.

3.9 Class monster

LEVEL   1+

AGE   4+

TIME   5 minutes +

AIMS   **To make words more memorable; to recycle words in a fun way; to develop sight vocabulary.**

MATERIALS   A monster poster (see Preparation), some poster paint and bath sponges, cards with words to feed the monster.

PREPARATION   1 Draw a big monster. Make the monster's mouth and stomach quite large, big enough to fit about ten word cards. You can either colour it beforehand or get the children to do it in class. You can cover a large area easily with poster paint and sponges.

2 Choose words you want the children to learn or revise and make cards with them on. Find pictures or flashcards of the items.

IN CLASS   1 Tell the children that the monster likes eating English words and that, as he or she is a monster, he or she eats anything: mountains, bananas, pizzas, plates, computers, etc.

2 Ask them to decide on a name for the monster.

3 Tell the children that he or she needs feeding in each English class, but that they can only feed him or her words they can remember.

4 Put some word cards on the board and keep the pictures in your hand.

5 Show the children a picture and tell them that if they can find the word on the board, they can feed it to the monster.

6 When they find the word, attach it to the monster's mouth.

7 Repeat this procedure until they have found all the words.

8 In the next lesson, show the children some pictures and see if they can match them to the word cards in the monster's mouth. The words they guess correctly move to the monster's stomach, as he has 'eaten' them. Any they have difficulty with stay in his mouth.

VARIATION 1

The children can make word and picture cards themselves, either in class or for homework.

VARIATION 2

You can make this activity more difficult by adding words that are similar, for example, if you have a picture of a *shirt*, make word cards for both *shirt* and *skirt*.

VARIATION 3

For children with a good vocabulary, you can choose words on a topic, for example, *Today the monster only wants to eat toys* or *...words starting with* f. For older children you could say that he only wants to eat triangular things, such as pyramids, mountains, a piece of pizza, or traffic signs.

FOLLOW-UP

Repeat Step 8 for five minutes in any lesson to recycle and revise vocabulary and spelling.

Acknowledgements
This activity is a writing version of the one in *Very Young Learners*, in this same series.

3.10 Meaningful copying

LEVEL

2+

AGE

7+

TIME

10 minutes

AIMS

To practise writing words; to make copying words more meaningful.

MATERIALS

A pencil and paper/notebook for each child.

IN CLASS

1 Choose a topic, for example, 'food', and elicit words from the children. List them on the board.

2 Tell the children that they are going to copy the words and categorize them, for example, healthy/unhealthy food, hot/cold food, food they like/don't like, fruit/vegetables.

3 Draw columns with headings on the board. Ask the children to do the same and then copy the words into the correct columns.

Examples of other categories

Clothes	winter/summer clothes; clothes you are wearing/not wearing at the moment; sportswear/swimwear
Animals	farm/zoo/domestic animals; animals that live on land/in water/both; animals with a tail/fur/scales/big ears; animals with no legs/two legs/four legs/four or more legs.
Colours	you like/don't like; primary/secondary colours; bright/dull, warm/cold
Sports	sports you play with a ball/sports you need other equipment for; safe/dangerous sports; sports you need/don't need to be very fit to play; sports you play alone/in teams
Verbs	school activities/out-of-school activities; things you do in the morning/afternoon; things you do on holiday/in term time.

3.11 Word-list races

LEVEL	2+
AGE	7+
TIME	**10 minutes +**
AIMS	**To write lists of words on a topic.**
MATERIALS	Paper and pencils.
IN CLASS	1 Elicit some of the topics covered in class.
	2 Write the topics on separate pieces of paper and put them in a bag.
	3 Divide the class into groups.
	4 Take out a piece of paper and read out the topic.
	5 The groups have two minutes to write down all the words they know on that topic. (You may want to give them more time depending on the level and age of the children.)
	6 They get two points per word. They only get one point if they make a spelling mistake.
VARIATION	Instead of topics you could place letters in the bag. The children take it in turns to pick letters and write a list of all the words they know which start with that letter.

3.12 Challenge!

LEVEL	2+
AGE	8+
TIME	30–40 minutes
AIMS	**To spell words correctly; to recognize words by their onset.**
MATERIALS	Resources for finding words and checking spelling, for example, dictionaries, word banks, word posters, a pencil and a sheet of paper per team, a board marker.

IN CLASS

1 Tell the children that you have thought of a word with four letters and that they are going to play a game to guess it. Write the first letter on the board. Explain that if they think they know the word, they must say *Challenge!* The first letter will probably not be challenged, so after a short wait write the second letter. Continue like this until someone has guessed the word or the whole word is revealed.

2 Divide the class into teams and tell them to think of a word they know with four letters. Ask them to keep it secret. Allow them to use resources in the classroom to check the spelling. Monitor for correct spelling, helping where necessary. The teams should appoint a secretary to write their word on the paper and later on the board.

3 Now divide the board into columns, one per team.

4 The secretary from Team 1 goes to the board and writes the first letter of their word in their column.

5 If a team guesses correctly, they win ten points, the word is added to their column, and it is their turn next.

6 If they do not guess correctly, the game continues. Team 1 gain five bonus points for each letter added to their word without the others guessing it. If no team guesses the word, Team 1 keep their word in their column and win 10 points plus all the bonus points. You decide which team plays next.

VARIATION

To make the game more difficult, allow the children to choose longer words.

FOLLOW-UP

At the end, challenge more experienced children to write a sentence using as many of the words from the board as possible.

COMMENTS

You have to be alert to who challenges first, as more than one team can challenge at the same time. If you think this will be noisy, you could give each team a card with the word *Challenge!* to hold up—this makes it quieter and easier to monitor.

3.13 A work of art: Arcimboldo

The children study one of Arcimboldo's paintings, in which he represents facial features with food and fruit. They use the idea to create their own picture and write words to describe it.

LEVEL

1+

AGE

7+

TIME

30 minutes + over two lessons

AIMS

To practise the vocabulary of faces, fruit, flowers, and vegetables in a memorable way; to link art and crafts with literacy.

MATERIALS

A copy of one of Arcimboldo's pictures of faces made from flowers, fruit or vegetables, especially *Spring*, *Summer*, or *Autumn*. Use a poster or art book, or download a picture from the Internet (see Further Reading). A piece of A4 paper for each child, glue, coloured paints, felt tips or pencils, and coloured chalk.

Summer by Giuseppe Arcimboldo (1573). Louvre, Paris

IN CLASS

1 Show the children the Arcimboldo face you have chosen. Point out the detail and show the children how the face is made up of fruit, flowers, and vegetables. Tell the children that he was a famous Italian painter in the 16th century. Tell them his name (Giuseppe Arcimboldo) and the title of the picture.

2 Now elicit all the appropriate vocabulary the children know and write it on the board. Alternatively, if you have a food word bank (see activity 3.1), elicit the vocabulary using the word cards.

3 Focusing on the painting again, elicit the parts of the face and write them on the board: *eyes, ears, mouth, nose, face, hair*. You could teach the children *cheeks* and *eyebrows* if you want more detail in the picture.

4 Model the activity. Ask the class to volunteer fruit or food for parts of the face. Draw the face on the board with coloured chalk, or let one or a number of children do the drawing.

5 You, or the children, label the face with the food vocabulary.

6 Give out the paper and let the children draw their own Arcimboldo-style faces. Monitor the children's progress and give praise for their creativity.

7 Tell the children to label the food in their picture.

8 Display the pictures in the classroom and let the children sign their pictures like real artists.

FOLLOW-UP

At sentence level, you may give the children the model: *I chose (food) for the (part of the face)* and encourage them to write a description of their picture. Read out some of the descriptions to the class and see if they can say which picture it is describing. Alternatively, give each child one of the descriptions and ask them to find the picture it is describing. You could provide a writing guide depending on what they have chosen (see the example).

I chose	oranges bananas an apple spaghetti grapes a tomato cherries a pineapple nuts	because	it they I	is are have got looks look	brown blue green yellow red spiky rosy round	like	blond hair a big red nose curly hair cheeks eyes lips earrings hair

Photocopiable © Oxford University Press

Older children with more experience can write about their picture and give reasons for their choices.

VARIATION

Another work of art which inspires rewarding language work is Van Gogh's *The Starry Night*. See Further Reading for websites with paintings and information.

Onset and rime activities

It is valuable to introduce children to the concept of **onset** and **rime**, even though we would not use these words with the children. Instead say: *Look how the word starts and how it ends.*

Onset and rime introduce children to the idea of **word families** and lays down foundations for good spelling strategies, as it practises the skill of applying rules across families.

'Rime' is different from 'rhyme': *rhyme* refers to the same sound, for example, *here* and *hear*, whereas *rime* refers to an identical string of letters which do not always make the same sound, for example, *ear*, *bear*.

3.14   Word family posters

LEVEL	1+
AGE	4+
TIME	**15–20 minutes**
AIMS	**To concentrate on rime (word endings); to help children to start recognizing word families; to enhance phonic knowledge.**
MATERIALS	Word cards, poster-size paper, coloured pens, magazines or drawing paper, scissors if using magazine pictures, something to attach the words to the board.
PREPARATION	Make cards of words with the same ending that the children know, for example, *bat, cat, fat, hat, rat, sat; bun, fun, gun, run, sun.* Write the rimes -*at* and -*un* at the top of the board. Draw columns for the word cards to be categorized.

IN CLASS

1 Show the children each word card and elicit or revise the meaning. Fix the cards in random order to the bottom of the board.

2 Point to each rime on the board and sound it out, for example, /æ/ /t/ → at.

3 Invite the children to find a word with the same letters at the end and come and take it from the board.

4 Ask what the word says. Point to the letters on the card and ask if they can put it in the correct column. Praise them if they can. If a child puts the word in the wrong column, repeat the rimes and try to get them to self-correct. If necessary, point to the correct column.

5 When all the words are sorted on the board in columns, divide the children into groups. Give each group a poster with a different rime.

6 Tell them to make posters copying each word in colour and using magazine pictures or drawings to illustrate them, and to help them remember the words. Display these as another kind of word bank.

VARIATION

Older children could make posters with more difficult words, for example, *dear, fear, hear, near, rear, tear, year; fight, light, might, night, right, sight, tight.*

FOLLOW-UP 1

Encourage the children to think of more words they know with the same rime and add them to the posters.

FOLLOW-UP 2

Store the cards in Rime word banks.

3.15 Word-forming spinners

LEVEL

1+

AGE

6+

TIME

15–20 minutes

AIMS

To focus on onset and rime.

MATERIALS

Spinners, dictionaries (optional), pen and paper for each child.

PREPARATION

Prepare two spinners, one with onsets and the other with rimes (see below for examples). You will need to make copies of these so that each group of children has one. Push a pencil through the centre of each spinner.

Examples:
rime: *it* onset: b, s, h, f, k
rime: *et* onset: j, l, n, m, p, w
rime: *at* onset: b, c, f, h, m, r
rime: *op* onset: h, m, t, and st (if you think it appropriate)
rime: *un* onset: b, f, g, r, s
rime: *an* onset: c, f, m, p, v

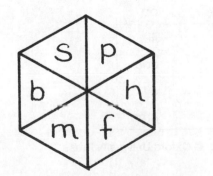 

IN CLASS

1 Divide the class into groups. Give each group an onset spinner and a rime spinner.

2 The children take it in turns to spin first the onset and then the rime spinner.

3 If a child is able to make a word, for example, using *m* and *an*, he or she writes it down.

4 The winner is the child who has made most words at the end.

3.16   Word fans

LEVEL

1+

AGE

6+

TIME

30 minutes

AIMS

To focus on the rime in words; to recognize word families; to reinforce vocabulary; to help children realize that some English words rhyme; to prepare for writing poetry (see Chapter 6).

MATERIALS

Large sheets of paper, alphabet flashcards, onset cards.

PREPARATION

Choose words the children know. Select or make cards with onsets and rimes to make words. Make some onsets with letter blends, for example, *pl*, *sp*. You may need more than one of each.

Here are some examples of onsets and rimes you could use:

onset	rime
d, f, l	og
b, f, g, r, s	un
t, w	alk
c, m, p, r, v	an
b, c, f, h, m, t, w	all
b, c, l, t, w	ake
h, p, st, t	op
f, h, p, w	ill
f, pl, sp	ace
d, m, pl, s, st, w	ay
c, f, g, n, s	ame

Photocopiable © Oxford University Press

IN CLASS

1 Demonstrate the activity by fixing a card with the rime *at* on the right-hand side of the board (or you could write it on the board). Put the onsets *b, c, f, h, th* in a line down the left-hand side of the board. Draw lines from the onsets to the rime and **sound out** each word you make: *bat, cat, fat, hat, that.* Draw an outline to look like a fan (see the illustration).

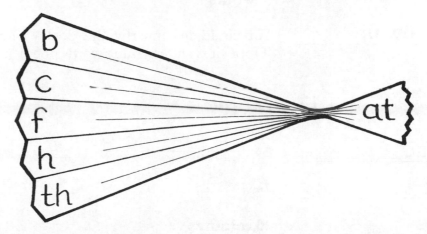

2 Write some rimes across the top of the board and draw columns for lists. Remind the children how to say each one.

3 Ask the children to find words in the room or think of words they know with the same rimes.

4 Give out onset cards.

5 Ask if anyone can make a word with their letter(s) and a word ending from the board. Let the children come and stand under the rime they need to make their word. Encourage the children to say their word, then write it under the rime on the board.

6 When all words are listed, give out the paper and show the children how to make a fan by folding the paper backwards and forwards to make a concertina shape.

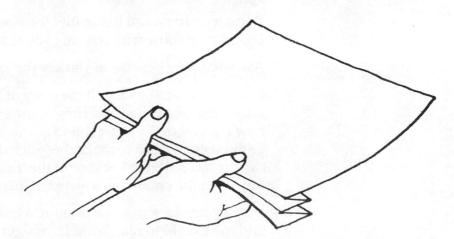

7 Finally, ask the children to choose a word family from the board and copy the words from the list, one in each fold of the fan, using a method like 3.3, 'Word windows/cameras' or 3.4, 'Look, say, cover, write, check'.

8 Display the fans or let the children keep them for reference when writing.

FOLLOW-UP   You could do some rhyming poetry with the children (see 6.3, 'Opposites and rhyming words poem').

3.17   Magic *e*

LEVEL   2+

AGE   7+

TIME   20 minutes

AIMS   **To learn the effect of the final *e* on spelling and pronunciation.**

MATERIALS   A magic wand, bought or made from a pencil with a star on the end, paper and pencils, highlighter pens or glitter pens.

IN CLASS   1 Write the following words on the board in two columns and read them aloud:

hop   hope
hat   hate
cut   cute
kit   kite
mad   made
tap   tape
not   note.

Point with the wand to identify the words with the short vowel sound then those with the long vowel sound as you read.

2 Ask what they hear when you say the second word.

3 Point to the final *e* and tell the story of 'magic *e*'—how it can make new words just by sitting at the end of them. Demonstrate how it changes the short sound in the first word into a long sound in the second word to make the letter say its name. The way we say the *a* is different because of the 'magic *e*' which sits very quietly at the end of the word and doesn't make a sound!

4 Play a game in which you point to a pair of words with your wand and ask a child to read both. If they get them correct say, *Magic!*

5 The children copy the words in the left-hand column. Give them a glitter pen or highlighter to write *e* on the end to create new words.

VARIATION 1	Prepare a list of words and ask the children to highlight or underline the vowel that is changed by the 'magic *e*', for example, *cake, bike, five, name*.
VARIATION 2	With more experienced children, teach the rule that when a word ends in a vowel plus a consonant plus *e*, the *e* is silent and the vowel is usually long, for example, *hope*. Exceptions: *have, give, come* and *move*.
VARIATION 3	With older children, introduce more complex words and ask the children to highlight the vowel affected by the *e*, for example, *escape, surprise, hopeless, exercise*.
COMMENTS	Exercise caution when teaching spelling rules: very few work consistently.

Rhyming activities

3.18　Sounds the same, looks different

LEVEL	1+
AGE	7+
TIME	20 minutes
AIMS	**To recognize rhyme; to use actions to aid recognition of rhyme; to practise auditory and visual memorization of words.**
MATERIALS	A rhyming chant, word cards of the rhyming words: two, shoe; four, door; six, sticks; eight, gate; ten, hen.
IN CLASS	1　Recite a rhyme with actions, for example:

One, two, buckle my shoe	*Count 1, 2 on your fingers and then pretend to buckle your shoe.*
Three, four, knock at the door	*Count 3, 4 then knock four times on the desk (or the door).*
Five, six, pick up sticks	*Count 5, 6 then pretend to pick up sticks from the floor.*
Seven, eight, close the gate	*Count 7, 8 and pretend to close a gate.*
Nine, ten, a big fat hen	*Hold up 9 then 10 fingers and mime a big fat hen*
Cluck! Cluck! Cluck!	*flapping its wings and pecking the ground.*

2 Ask ten children to come to the front. Give out the word cards. Tell the children to stand next to their rhyming partner. Ask them to place the cards on the floor and explain that when they hear their rhyming word, they must mime the action.

3 Have the class recite with you, shouting out the rhyming words.

4 Take each pair of words and point out how the letters make the same sound but look different.

5 The children copy the rhyming pairs, highlighting the letters which create the rhyme.

FOLLOW-UP

The children write an alternative nursery rhyme in pairs or groups but using different rhyming words, for example:

One, two, I see you
Three, four, sit on the floor
Five, six, do high kicks
Seven, eight, I can skate
Nine, ten, start again.

Let them perform it for the class.

Bridging the gap between phonics and word recognition

3.19   Word chains

LEVEL

1+

AGE

6+

TIME

10 minutes

AIMS

To identify letters and their corresponding sounds; to recognize letter patterns in words; to recognize words with the same visual pattern.

MATERIALS

Letter cards: *a, n, d, h, s.*

IN CLASS

1 Place letter *a* on the board and ask the children to say the letter sound.

2 Add letter *n* to make a new word. Ask the children the sound of the new letter, and then to read the new word.

3 Keep adding letters to make new words. Each time the children should say the new letter sound and read the new word, for example, *a, an, and, hand, hands.*

FOLLOW-UP

Repeat the activity in reverse. Write a word on the board and remove a letter at a time. Ask the children to name each letter sound as you remove it and read the new word, for example:

that, hat, at, a
diner, dine, din, in, I.

VARIATION

The children could look for letter patterns by searching for short words in longer words. The new words must have the letters in the same order as in the original word, for example, *important, port, or, tan, an, ant,* other possibilities are *imp* and *import*.

4 Sentence level

Although there are significant differences between spoken and written language, most children who can express themselves in words and sentences are ready to begin writing sentences. The vocabulary the children acquired at word level has far greater significance when they can write down whole chunks of language as a sentence and recognize it as English.

The best approach to writing at sentence level is to see it as very closely linked to word and text level. It is not necessary to work on each stage individually. Some activities from word level can be used to introduce many of the activities at sentence and text level: for example, 3.10, 'Meaningful copying', helps children to produce their own key word bank before attempting to write. This idea could be used to brainstorm and categorize vocabulary as an introduction to any writing activity. However, children must learn that sentences have certain grammatical features and need help in recognizing how correct syntax and punctuation will improve their writing and make it easier to read.

This chapter concentrates first on children writing simple sentences, using capital letters and full stops correctly. Later activities encourage creating and punctuating more complex sentences, focusing on the organization of words in a sentence and introducing clauses, as in 4.10, 'The longest sentence'. Direct speech is introduced by writing speech bubbles for characters in a picture, 4.12, 'Pictures come alive'. The parsing activities in 4.1, 'Traffic-light colour parsing', and 4.2, 'Dinosaur colour parsing', are designed to increase knowledge of parts of speech, sentence construction, and how to enhance writing with adjectives and adverbs. Towards the end of the chapter, 4.15, 'My life in a box', requires children to begin to form a basic text by using link words joining short sentences and using descriptive phrases.

Support for children as they write

Children need to see examples of what you want them to write, so modelling the process for them in **shared writing** activities is a feature of this chapter in order to teach the processes of good writing before they embark on their own writing. The teacher and children compose together whilst the teacher models the writing process on the board, guiding and editing. During shared writing the teacher and children talk about how sentences are formed, choose appropriate vocabulary, and discuss how punctuation is used to enhance their writing. Used effectively, this leads children towards greater independence by equipping them with skills they can mimic when writing on their own. Shared writing activities feature in 4.6, 'Living sentences', 4.12, 'Pictures come alive', and 4.14, 'Friendship tree'.

Another support for children is 'guided writing', when the teacher advises about structure and vocabulary, as in 4.9, 'Design a T-shirt', and in a more structured way in 4.7, 'Funny forfeits', which uses a **writing frame** to guide the children.

Writing in pairs or groups to generate ideas and compose together provides mutual support, and may help to build confidence before attempts at **independent writing**. 4.4, 'Sentence-level spinners', for example, is designed to help children to help each other to make sense of the task.

Making writing personal

Children enjoy writing about things that have personal meaning to them rather than topics dictated by the teacher. Initially, it is necessary to teach the concept of how to write a simple sentence, but once the children have grasped the idea, allow plenty of opportunities for them to write about their own experience, themselves and people they know. When the children are practising writing sentences in messages to each other, friends, and family members in 4.14, 'Friendship tree', it becomes a very personal piece of writing.

Talking for writing

This pre-writing strategy uses an 'oral rehearsal' activity for children to try out their ideas using the words, phrases, and sentences they need before they begin to write, which makes them more confident about tackling the task. It is a way of creating a mental word bank for them to draw upon as they write. Combined with a 'shared writing' session, this will provide a solid framework for writing their ideas.

No single teaching style suits all children, yet we must try to cater for all types of learners in class. Therefore, we need a balance of activities to teach children partly in the style they prefer, so that overall the needs of all children are met. With this in mind, we have designed ideas to appeal to different learning styles involving, for example, **Total Physical Response (TPR)** in 4.7, 'Funny forfeits'; physically making up a sentence with children in 4.6, 'Living sentences'; movement in 4.8, 'Running dictation'; the use of colour in 4.1 and 4.2, linking learning with things children like, for example, dinosaurs and pop stars. There is a visual effect and movement in 4.3, 'Leaf sentences'. 4.9, 'Design a T-shirt', combines writing and art with the satisfaction of creating something to wear.

4.5, 'Sentence flap books', involves some basic craft, whilst writing becomes a game in 4.4, 'Sentence-level spinners', and 4.10, 'The longest sentence'. Children can have fun with mime in 4.13, 'Nonsense rhymes', and there is movement and a tactile element in 4.11, 'Mixed bag'.

Not all children like writing about imaginary situations and prefer to connect their writing with real-life experiences. They may be imaginative in that they have good ideas but are unable to write about imaginary people and places, so it is important to give choices to include both the imagined and the real world for children who prefer more factual writing. Activities such as 4.15, 'My life in a box', and 4.16, 'Advertisements', may cater for such learners.

Word order

4.1 Traffic-light colour parsing

LEVEL	1+
AGE	7+
TIME	**20 minutes**
AIMS	**To make word order more memorable to the children; to show that the personal pronoun 'I' is written with a capital letter.**
MATERIALS	Red, yellow, and green chalk or board markers, 'traffic lights'.
PREPARATION	Make some traffic lights from three large circles of coloured card: red, yellow, and green. Prepare some simple sentences with structures you want the children to practise, for example, a subject pronoun, verb, and noun as object. Write the pronouns in the red circle, the verbs in the yellow circle, and the nouns in the green circle.
IN CLASS	1 Elicit the colours of traffic lights and which order they light up in.

2 Write a simple sentence on the board, for example, *I like sausages*. Ask the children to look at the traffic lights and see which words are in which colour. Rub out each word in your sentence and write it in the colour the children tell you.

3 Establish that the red words are the ones like *I, you, he, she, it, you, we, they*, the yellow words are ones like *play, like, eat*, and the green words are ones like *sausages, tennis*, etc.

4 Ask the children to make sentences, taking the first word from

the red traffic light, the second from the yellow, and the ⟨
from the green. If they have learnt this, remind the chil⟨
when the red word is *he/she/it* the green word finishes in *s*.

VARIATION 1
Divide the children into groups. The first group to make a correct sentence gets a point.

VARIATION 2
The groups prepare lists of words for other groups to sort into the colour parsing sets. The children could write them in their books in colour.

FOLLOW-UP
When correcting sentences in class, use the colour parsing coding to show where the children may have gone wrong. Help the children locate the problem: for example, is it a problem with meaning (for example, *I play sausages*), or word order (*The traffic-light colours are in the wrong order*), or a problem with a particular word (for example, *The verb is missing an* s)?

COMMENTS
There is no need to mention the terms *pronoun*, *verb*, and *noun* to the children at this stage.

4.2 Dinosaur colour parsing

LEVEL
1+

AGE
7+

TIME
25 minutes

AIMS
To make word order more memorable; to demonstrate how to write in sentences; to add descriptive words (adjectives) to make sentences more interesting; to show that the personal pronoun 'I' is a capital letter.

MATERIALS
The dinosaurs from the illustrations below.

Photocopiable © Oxford University Press

PREPARATION

Make the dinosaurs by enlarging the illustrations above and colouring each one, so that they are more memorable to the children, for example, a red Pronounosaurus, a yellow Verbosaurus, a blue Adjectivosaurus, and a green Nounosaurus. Alternatively, copy each one on to different coloured paper/card. Prepare some sentences with words to go with each dinosaur—include pronouns, verbs, nouns, and adjectives.

IN CLASS

1 Introduce the students to the red Pronounosaurus and say: *My name's Pronounosaurus and I like words like 'I'*. Attach the dinosaur to the board and write the word 'I' below. If you used traffic-light parsing with the group, remind them that they are red words.

2 Next, show the children the yellow Verbosaurus. Say: *My name's Verbosaurus and I like words like 'eat'*. Attach the dinosaur to the board, next to the Pronounosaurus and write the word 'eat' below it.

3 Show the children the green Nounosaurus and say: *I like words like 'apples'*. Attach the dinosaur in the line but leave a space for the Adjectivosaurus.

4 Read the sentence pointing to each word as you say it: *I like apples*.

5 Now show them the blue Adjectivosaurus and tell them he likes words like 'big' and 'red'. Attach the dinosaur before the Nounosaurus and write 'big' and 'red'. Now read the sentence— *I eat big, red apples*. Ask the children why the blue Adjectivosaurus goes in front of the green Nounosaurus and try and elicit that it is because it describes the green word and so they are linked. You could make these two dinosaurs face each other.

6 Now write the sentences you prepared as random words all over the board.

7 Ask the children which words the Pronounosaurus would like and invite different children to come and circle the word with a green chalk/pen. Then write the words under the dinosaur.

8 Repeat the procedure for all the other words, using different coloured chalk/pens for each group.

9 Invite the children to make sentences, choosing a word from each dinosaur group and writing the sentence in their notebooks.

10 Display the dinosaurs, updating the word bank from time to time to reflect current vocabulary.

FOLLOW-UP

Just as word banks are a strategy for helping with spelling, the dinosaurs can become the children's sentence writing strategy. Once the children start to write more complex sentences, create new dinosaurs.

VARIATION	For older children you could replace dinosaur cut-outs with pop stars cut-outs. Instead of dinosaurs, draw pop stars dressed in the colour parsing coding, for example, *Pippi Pronoun is in red, Vicki Verb is in yellow, Andy Adjective is in blue, Niki Noun is in green, and Adele Adverb is in purple.*
FOLLOW-UP 1	Divide the children into groups and tell them they have to make a sentence from the different colour parsing sets. The first group to make a correct sentence gets a point.
FOLLOW-UP 2	The different groups prepare lists for other groups to sort into the colour parsing sets. The children could write them in their books in colour.
FOLLOW-UP 3	When correcting sentences in class, use the colour parsing coding to show where the children may have gone wrong. Help the children locate the problem by showing them if it was a problem with word order, for example, the dinosaur/pop star is in the wrong place, or where it is a problem with a particular word, for example, *Vicki Verb is missing an* s *or is in the wrong tense.*

4.3 Leaf sentences

LEVEL	1+
AGE	7+
TIME	10–15 minutes
AIMS	**To help with word order in a sentence, and to make word order more memorable; to recognize that a sentence contains a complete thought.**
MATERIALS	Card in various colours to make the leaves; something to attach the 'leaves' to the board.
PREPARATION	1 Select a structure you want to practise and prepare some sentences, for example, *I like tennis and football. He likes bread and butter. She likes cartoon films.*
	2 Cut out some leaves in different colours, for example, red for pronouns, yellow for verbs, orange for conjunctions, and green for nouns. Write the words from the sentences you prepared on the corresponding coloured leaves.
IN CLASS	1 Draw a tree trunk on the board and attach the leaves to form a tree shape.
	2 Tell the children that they need to form sentences and make the leaves fall from the tree in the correct order.

3   Do one sentence with the class. Draw the children's attention to the colour coding. (You do not need to refer to the words as *verb*, *pronoun*, etc. You could just say *a yellow word, a red word*, and so on.)

4   Now ask the children, either individually or in pairs, to come to the board and make sentences. As they remove the leaves from the tree, they should place them in a line below. They can choose any words and do not have to form exactly the same sentences as long as they make sense.

5   Encourage the children to write their own sentences, personalizing the information, for example, what they like or what their friend likes.

COMMENTS

The activity will get easier as the words are used up as there will be fewer to choose from each time.

FOLLOW-UP

Once the children have used up all the leaves in the sentences, children with a higher level of English can make new sentences by choosing other pronouns and nouns they know, paying attention to whether the pronoun agrees with the verb in their new sentence.

4.4 Sentence-level spinners

LEVEL

1+

AGE

6+

TIME

30 minutes

AIMS

To make word order memorable; to recognize that a sentence contains a complete thought.

MATERIALS

Three spinners in the shape of hexagons for each group of children (see 3.15, 'Word-forming spinners'), a photocopy of Worksheet 4.4 for each child.

IN CLASS

1   On Spinner 1, tell the children to colour each segment a different colour and write in the names of the colours. On Spinner 2 they write *body, head, arms, legs, feet, hands*. On Spinner 3 they write *ears, eye, mouth, nose, hair, face*.

2   Now give out Worksheet 4.4.

3   The children take it in turns to spin Spinner 1 and then one of the other spinners. They then dictate to the group: for example, *a blue leg*, and everyone colours.

4   Remind the children always to use Spinner 1 first, so that they remember that the adjective goes first.

5   Once they have finished they write a description, for example, *My clown has a blue nose, green ears, a purple mouth, and pink hair.*

4.5 Sentence flap books

LEVEL	2+
AGE	7+
TIME	40 minutes +
AIMS	**To practise sentence structure; to look at grammar in simple sentences.**

MATERIALS A4 or letter-size paper and staplers. An example of a sentence flap book.

PREPARATION Make an example of a sentence flap book:
1 Fold several sheets of paper in half and staple them in a line about 1cm in from the folded edge.
2 Cut the book into three sections from the open edge to the stapled spine, to make the flaps.
3 Write simple sentences consisting of a pronoun, verb, and noun, for example, *I like bananas. She likes tennis. They play basketball.* Make sure that the pronoun is in the top flap, the verb in the middle, and the noun at the bottom.

IN CLASS
1 Show the children the flap book and show them how they can make different sentences by opening the flaps on different pages to change pronouns, verbs, and nouns.

2 The children make their own sentence flap books. The first time they could copy your sentences. Then you dictate new sentences and the children have to find the sentence by opening different flaps and show it to you.

3 They invent their own sentences to dictate to their partners.

COMMENTS

You may need to remind the children that the third person verb has an *s* on the end in the simple present by showing them an incorrect sentence and encouraging them to tell you what is wrong, for example, *★He like football.*

FOLLOW-UP

The children can make other sentence flap books with their own sentences. Once they are writing more complicated sentences, they could make books with four or five flaps per page.

4.6   Living sentences

LEVEL

2+

AGE

7+

TIME

40 minutes +

AIMS

To practise sentence structure, and to move towards an awareness of parts of speech; to recognize that a sentence contains a complete thought.

MATERIALS

A picture, photo, or reproduction of a painting you think might interest the children. In our example we have chosen Henri Rousseau's *The Tropics*, as most children like his paintings and this activity could lead to a freer writing activity.

PREPARATION

Write some sentences describing the picture and write each word on a separate card big enough for the class to see. Write the first word with a capital letter and include the full stop with the last word of each sentence. The sentences about this picture might read:

There are four monkeys. A big brown monkey is sitting on a branch. Two red monkeys are sitting in the grass. Two monkeys are eating oranges.

IN CLASS

1 Look at the picture and ask the children what they can see. *How many monkeys are there?* The children may just spot four. *Can you find a hidden monkey? What kind of trees are there?* Teach any words they might need, for example, *branch, orange, near, behind.*

2 Show the children the word cards of one of the sentences which describe the scene:

| monkeys. | five | There | are |

3 Encourage the children to work out the word order. Remind them that in English we start sentences with a capital letter and finish with a full stop. This will help the children to find the first and last words.

4 Give each card to a child and ask them to stand at the front in the correct sentence order, letting the rest of the class guide them.

5 Once they are in the correct order, display the cards where the whole class can see them.

6 Repeat the procedure with another sentence, for example, *A big brown monkey is sitting on a branch.* You could help the children with the word order by asking questions such as: *Can you see a word that is a person or thing? (monkey, tree).* The children with 'monkey' and 'tree' come and stand at the front. *Can you see any words that tell us more about the monkey? (big, brown).* The children holding 'big' and 'brown' hold hands and go and stand before the child holding 'monkey'. The child with 'brown' puts his/her left arm around the child with 'monkey' to demonstrate that two adjectives support the noun. Repeat the procedure for the present continuous verb 'sitting'. Work through the other words, asking the children: *Where is the monkey sitting?* and indicate that the child with the word 'tree' should move to the end of the line.

7 Repeat the procedure for all the sentences.

8 Read through the sentences and invite children to come and point to the part of the picture each describes.

The Tropics by Henri Rousseau. Private Collection.

FOLLOW-UP 1

Ask the children to close their eyes. Remove some of the word cards and see if they can remember the words.

FOLLOW-UP 2

Change the order of some of the word cards and see if the children can spot the error. You could make this into a game where one group closes their eyes whilst another group changes the word order or removes a card for the other group to solve.

FOLLOW-UP 3

The children draw pictures on a similar theme and write captions describing their pictures.

COMMENTS

If you have done colour parsing with your class (see 4.1–4.3), you could use the colour references.

4.7   Funny forfeits

LEVEL

2+

AGE

8+

TIME

30 minutes +

AIMS

To practise imperatives and use them to give instructions.

MATERIALS

Paper or notebooks, pencils, a die for each group.

PREPARATION

Prepare lists of instructions. Number each instruction 1–6 (see the example). You will have to vary the instructions depending on the age and level of your students.

IN CLASS

1 Play a simple **Total Physical Response** activity, giving the children simple instructions to follow. You could play 'Simon says' (see 2.7 in *Very Young Learners* in this series) or make some instructions into a chant or a song to a tune the children know, for example, 'Bobby Shaftoe'.

Touch your nose and touch your toes. (x 3)
Early in the morning.
Wave your arms and stamp your feet …
Shake your hands and wiggle your fingers …
Shake your body and touch your tummy …
Bend your knees and lift your shoulders …

Touch your toes

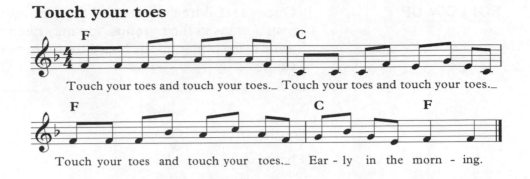

Touch your toes and touch your toes.＿ Touch your toes and touch your toes.＿

Touch your toes and touch your toes.＿ Ear - ly in the morn - ing.

2 Divide the class into groups of four or five. Give each group a list and a die.

3 Each group takes it in turns to throw the die and do the corresponding instruction.

List 1	List 2	List 3
1 Shake your head. 2 Touch your toes. 3 Wave your fingers. 4 Be a rabbit. 5 Touch your nose. 6 Close your eyes and pretend to eat a banana.	1 Touch your ears and stamp your feet. 2 Pat your tummy. 3 Stamp your feet and shake your head. 4 Eat an ice-cream. 5 Be a bird. 6 Point to something blue.	1 Eat an apple. 2 Be an elephant. 3 Close your eyes and stand on one leg. 4 Wash your face. 5 Comb your hair. 6 Touch your nose with your tongue.
List 4	**List 5**	**List 6**
1 Be a turtle. 2 Pat your legs. 3 Wave your arms and stamp your feet. 4 Be a robot. 5 Open and close your mouth like a fish. 6 Eat a banana.	1 Open your mouth. 2 Be a spider. 3 Play a noisy trumpet. 4 Stamp your feet and pat your tummy. 5 Wave your arms and open your mouth. 6 Touch your knee with your nose.	1 Point to something yellow and stand on one leg. 2 Pretend to talk on the phone. 3 Close your eyes. 4 Eat a banana. 5 Close your eyes and touch your nose with your finger. 6 Wave your fingers.

Photocopiable © Oxford University Press

FOLLOW UP

1 Once the children understand the activity, they write a list of instructions in their groups. You may need to help the children by writing examples on the board for them to choose from, for example:

		head					
Touch		nose					hand.
Shake		knee					fingers.
Wiggle		body	extras	with	your		nose.
Bend	your	eyes					
Stamp		ears					
Close		mouth					
Point to		feet					
Wink		fingers					
		toes					

	a monster.
	an elephant.
Pretend to be …	a train.
Pretend to eat …	a plane.
Move like …	a witch.
	a ghost.
	a banana.

2 Once the groups have finished their lists, each group teams up with another group and throws the die. They say the number they have thrown and read out the instruction for the other group to act out. They get a point for each correct action.

Listen and write

4.8 Running dictation

LEVEL	2+
AGE	7+
TIME	20 minutes
AIMS	**To encourage children to write down what they hear; to practise careful pronunciation.**
MATERIALS	A number of short texts: a poem, a joke, a riddle, a song, a funny story, or English you would like the children to revise; paper and pencils.
PREPARATION	Write or print the texts onto cards and position the cards around the classroom.

IN CLASS

1 Draw the children's attention to the cards on the walls.

2 Divide the children into pairs, A and B.

3 Tell the children that B must get up, read the text on the wall, then go back and dictate it to A. They can go back as many times as necessary to get all the words. Demonstrate if necessary.

4 Tell them that B must sit down next to A before he or she speaks, otherwise they are out of the game. This is to stop B from standing by the text and shouting it to A.

5 Change the roles so that everyone gets the opportunity to dictate and to write.

6 When they have finished, check the English.

VARIATION   Make it into a competition and award points to the winners.

Building and writing sentences

4.9   Design a T-shirt

LEVEL	1+
AGE	7+
TIME	**40–60 minutes over two lessons**
AIMS	**To provide the children with an interesting outcome for their writing.**

MATERIALS   Plain T-shirts (new T-shirts should be washed first), felt-tip fabric pens or fabric crayons. If it is not possible to use T-shirts, you could use paper or fabric.

PREPARATION   Find some T-shirts with writing, slogans, and pictures on for the children to look at. Tell the children to bring, or wear to class, any T-shirts with writing, especially in English, if this is permitted in school.

IN CLASS

1 Spend a short time looking at and talking about the commercially produced T-shirts you and your children have brought to class, focusing on colour, design, style of writing, and the slogans.

2 Tell the children that they are going to create a design and transfer it to a T-shirt.

3 Ask the children to think of ideas for a message which they want on their T-shirt. For example, messages about saving the environment or descriptions such as *A good friend is …* work well. Younger children could draw and label things they like to eat, for example, *I like apples. Yum! Yum!* or draw their pet and write a sentence about it, for example, *I love hamsters.*

4 Give the children a piece of paper to design their T-shirt.

5 **(Optional)** When you have made corrections and suggestions, the children transfer their information on to the T-shirts. The best way to do this is with pens, paints, or crayons that are specially designed for drawing and writing on fabric.

COMMENTS

1 Insert a piece of cardboard in the middle of the T-shirt to prevent the colour from going through to the other side and to provide a surface to work on.

2 If there is a slogan for both the front and back of the T-shirt, allow one side to dry before turning to write on the other side.

3 Each child should work at their own level and use their personal talents, some writing more, others using drawing and writing, some doing annotated cartoons.

4.10 The longest sentence

LEVEL

2+

AGE

8+

TIME

20 minutes

AIMS

To practise writing in sentences, and to use the term 'sentence' appropriately; to reinforce use of capital letters and full stops, and to begin to use commas when punctuating sentences.

PREPARATION

Prepare word banks (see 3.1) or ensure that existing word banks are updated to include recent vocabulary.

IN CLASS

1 Divide the class into groups.

2 Tell the children that you are going to write a sentence on the board and that each group is going to try to extend the sentence. They will get points for the number of words they use and will be awarded extra points for using long but appropriate words. Tell the children that the sentence must always make sense.

3 Give each group a copy of the word bank if you think they need help as we are not necessarily practising how many words they can remember, but how well they use them.

Suggested scoring system for each new word added:

Someone's name	1 point
a/an, the, as, and, 2-letter words	2 points
words with 3/4 letters	3 points
words with 5 letters	4 points
words with 6 or more letters	5 points

4 Do a trial run. Example (for pre-intermediate children):

Original sentence: I saw a boy on a bike.

> _Yesterday_, I saw a boy on a bike.
> Yesterday, I saw a _small_ boy on a bike.
> Yesterday, I saw a small boy on a _new_ bike.
> Yesterday, I saw a small boy on a _beautiful_, new bike.
> Yesterday, I saw a small boy _called John_, on a beautiful, new bike.
> Yesterday afternoon, I saw a small boy called John, on a beautiful new, _red_ bike.
> Yesterday _afternoon_, I saw a small boy called John _riding_ on a beautiful new, red bike.
> Yesterday afternoon, I saw a small boy called John riding _in the park_ on a beautiful new, red bike.

5 Let the children try other sentences.

4.11   Mixed bag

LEVEL	2+
AGE	7+
TIME	**20–30 minutes (depending on the number of objects)**
AIMS	**To encourage children to create sentences.**
MATERIALS	A bag of objects the children know in English from different topic areas, some thick markers or board markers. Alternatively, you could use a bag with flashcards.
PREPARATION	Prepare some large strips of paper.
IN CLASS	

1 Take the objects out one at a time and elicit the names. To revise the words, you could play 1.5, 'Kim's game'.

2 Show each object and brainstorm linked words, for example, _tiger—orange_, _black_, _jungle_, _wild_, _roar_.

3 Put all the objects back in the bag.

4 Divide the class into groups and ask each group to come and take out two objects without looking.

5 The groups then try and write a sentence linking the two objects, for example, _The orange and black tiger drives a big yellow car._ Go round monitoring the children's progress, making any corrections needed.

6 The groups write their sentences on the strips of paper, using a thick marker.

7 Collect the objects and put them where the whole class can see them, mixing them up.

8 Collect the sentences and give them out to different groups.

9 Each group reads their sentence and finds the objects.

10 The children pick again and write another sentence.

FOLLOW-UP

The children draw pictures with their sentences as captions.

4.12 Pictures come alive

The children create a dialogue between characters in pictures. They write out the spoken words on cut-out speech bubbles and glue them to the pictures.

LEVEL

2+

AGE

7+

TIME

30 minutes

AIMS

To introduce direct speech; to create simple dialogues.

Photocopiable © Oxford University Press

MATERIALS

A large poster-sized picture with lots of activity, smaller pictures (from magazines) which lend themselves to an imaginary conversation, for example, families in the park, a birthday party. You will need one picture for each pair of children. Glue, 'Blu-tack' (sticky putty), or something easily removable to fix the speech bubbles to the pictures.

PREPARATION

Cut out some speech bubble shapes from card (older children could do this themselves).

IN CLASS

1 Show the large picture and ask the children to describe what is happening.

2 Explore every angle before embarking upon what the characters might be saying to each other. Elicit information, such as *Where are they? Is it a nice day? What are they doing?*

3 Ask the children to imagine what the characters are saying to each other.

4 Teach or revise the way we indicate the spoken word in writing. Demonstrate on the board with inverted commas and a speech bubble. Write some examples of dialogue from the large picture.

5 Now write the words in the speech bubbles and fix them to the picture.

6 Put the children in pairs and give out the magazine pictures to each pair.

7 Ask them to imagine what the characters may be saying to each other and write it out on draft paper.

8 Give out the speech bubbles and tell the children to write out neatly what the characters are saying and then glue the speech bubbles in the best position on the picture.

9 Let them go round and read each other's work.

VARIATION

Choose a series of pictures on the same topic. Have the children sort them into the order of a possible story and write speech bubbles. Stick the pictures in order and display them. Make a class book of the picture stories.

4.13 Nonsense rhymes

In this activity the rhyme matters more than an identical rime.

LEVEL

2+

AGE

7+

TIME

20–30 minutes

AIMS

To recognize which words rhyme; to write sentences and illustrate them.

MATERIALS

A pair of rhyming words on cards for each pair of children.

PREPARATION

Make the word cards. It is a good idea to make extra cards so that if some children cannot make a sentence, you can give them another pair of words.

IN CLASS

1 Put the children in pairs and give out the cards.

2 Tell them they must read the rhyming words and try to think of a sentence linking the two words, for example:

   snake/cake—A snake is eating cake.
   hen/pen—A hen is writing with a pen.

3 The children draft possible sentences and check them with you.

4 They choose the best one to write out and illustrate.

FOLLOW-UP 1

The children could act out rhymes, for example:

Run for a bun	*Run and pick up a bun.*
Skip to the ship	*Skip towards a picture of a ship.*
Cat in a hat	*Pretend to stroke your whiskers and pull on a hat with both hands.*
Ball in the hall	*Pretend to bounce a ball.*
Make a cake	*Beat the mixture.*
Tea for me	*Pretend to sip tea and point to yourself.*
See the sea	*Shade your eyes with your hand and look from side to side and make 'wave' movements with your hand.*

FOLLOW-UP 2

The children mime or act out funny rhyming sentences and other children guess what they are.

4.14 Friendship tree

Children write messages to each other and hang them on a tree made from twigs in a vase. This is an ongoing activity as the children can change the messages regularly.

LEVEL

2+

AGE

7+

TIME

20–30 minutes

AIMS

To practise sentence formation; to practise vocabulary and functions, such as expressing a reason, for example, *I like you because ...*

MATERIALS

Twigs, a vase or similar container, card, pencils, felt-tip pens, scissors, a hole punch, string, gift ribbon or brightly coloured wool.

PREPARATION

Make a small tree from twigs and secure it in the container. Make some sample messages and hang them on the tree. Make sure the word bank/wall contains suitable vocabulary. Prepare some pieces of card for children to write their messages on.

IN CLASS

1 Talk about friends and best friends. Ask the children why we like our friends and encourage responses such as: *because she smiles a lot, because he plays with me, because he makes me laugh, because we play football together.* Write examples on the board.

2 Extend this if you wish to include family members, for example, *I love my Mum because she loves me, … my Dad because he tells me jokes, … my Grandma because she makes my favourite food.*

3 Model a sentence, for example, *I like my friend because she is always happy.*

4 Put the children in pairs and ask them to tell their partner why they like their friend.

5 Help them to draft a sentence about their friend.

6 Give each child a piece of card or paper for them to copy their sentence.

7 Make holes in the cards, thread them with wool or ribbon, and hang them on the tree.

VARIATION

On Valentine's Day the children send their friends messages written on red hearts.

FOLLOW-UP

This can be a permanent feature of the class. You could write messages to the children about special events, for example:

Well done to Anna because she was brave at the dentist.
Thank you Jaime because you helped me when I hurt my knee.
Best wishes to Sarah and her new baby brother.
Happy birthday, Robert. He is 9 today.

The children can then use your messages as models to write greetings to each other.

COMMENTS

You could prepare this activity for International Friendship Day, which is the first Sunday in August. If this falls in holiday time, the children could do the activity beforehand and take the messages they make home to their family ready for International Friendship Day.

4.15 My life in a box

LEVEL	**2+**
AGE	**8+**
TIME	**30 minutes + over two lessons**
AIMS	**To help children to write sentences about themselves.**
MATERIALS	Each child needs a shoe box or a medium-sized box with a lid.
PREPARATION	You will need to plan well in advance for this activity as the children need to bring things from home. It is best to send a note home asking for the children to bring a shoe box with items special to them, for example, photos of family and pets, a favourite book or toy. If something is too precious or big to fit in the box, they could do a drawing.

IN CLASS

1 The children draft a sentence about each thing in the box. You could give them model sentences to complete, for example, *My … is very special because my … bought it for me. I like this book because … .*

2 Check for any mistakes.

3 Tell the children that they are going to display their box as if in a museum and they must do their best writing to stick next to their 'exhibit'.

4 Remind the children that as in a museum, they are not allowed to touch one another's things, just look.

5 They can ask each other questions about the things in the boxes.

4.16 Advertisements

LEVEL	**2+**
AGE	**9+**
TIME	**30 minutes +**
AIMS	**To write slogans; to think about advertising methods.**
MATERIALS	Pictures of famous people your children know and a list of products for the people to advertise, examples of adverts, magazines with pictures, scissors, and glue.

PREPARATION

1 In a previous lesson, find out which famous personalities your children know. Look for pictures of some of these people in newspapers and magazines. Choose products for them to endorse.

2 Make product and famous people cards like the following:

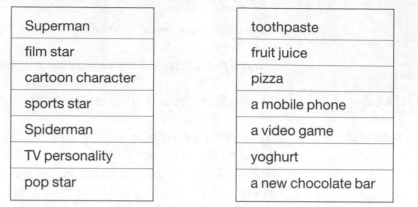

Superman		toothpaste
film star		fruit juice
cartoon character		pizza
sports star		a mobile phone
Spiderman		a video game
TV personality		yoghurt
pop star		a new chocolate bar

3 Find examples of adverts with famous people, either in the children's mother tongue or in English.

IN CLASS

1 Talk to the children about how famous people are paid by companies to say they use their products. Ask them if they think this is a good way of selling products and why.

2 Ask whether they buy things because famous people advertise them.

3 Look at some adverts with famous people and talk about the language in the slogans.

4 Divide the class into groups.

5 One child from each group comes out and takes a famous person card and a product card.

6 The children look through magazines to find adverts and cut out any useful pictures.

7 Tell them they need to choose a name for their product and think of a slogan. Go around the class, drawing their attention to any links between the person and the product and assist with slogans.

8 The children choose other pictures for background illustrations and cut them out. They produce their posters, arranging the slogan and the pictures.

9 Display the posters and allow the children time to read each other's adverts.

VARIATION

The children can also do a TV version with a dialogue and act it out.

4.17   Alliterative sentences

LEVEL	2+
AGE	9+
TIME	15+

AIMS

To write short alliterative sentences; to aid pronunciation; to enjoy the unusual sounds of alliteration.

PREPARATION

Write or choose some examples of sentences where most of the words begin with the same letter or sound.

IN CLASS

1 Show the children the following sentence: *Ellie the elephant eats eggs in the evenings.*

2 Ask what is unusual about the sentence (answer: all the main words begin with the same letter).

3 Show the children some more examples of alliterative sentences:
   Smooth snakes slide silently.
   Busy Brenda buys bananas by the bunch.
   Silly Sarah wears sweaters on sunny summer days.
   Perfect Peter plays the piano perfectly.

4 Draw four bubble shapes on the board.

5 Now elicit some verbs and write them in one of the bubbles.

6 Next, elicit nouns and names, encouraging the children to find some starting with the same letters as some of the verbs.

7 Repeat this procedure for adjectives.

8 Divide the class into pairs and encourage them to choose a word beginning with the same letter from each bubble to make a sentence.

FOLLOW-UP 1

See if the children can create sentences for other letters in the alphabet.

FOLLOW-UP 2

Children can make an alliterative book with a new page for each letter. This can be added to at any time when the children write a new sentence or poem.

5 Text level

Text level is a critical stage in children's growing independence as writers as there is an important relationship between the ability to write well and success in English. For children to be successful, writing skills learned so far must be practised and consolidated but in new and motivational ways. Activities in this unit cover many scenarios from describing the vivid paintings of Van Gogh, researching family history, winning words to write stories, listening to music to conjure up distant places and people, and writing about favourite celebrities. Whether they are exciting, mysterious, funny, true to life, or imaginary, the primary aims of these activities are enjoyment and getting children actively involved in writing.

What is text?

It is important for children to understand the concept of text. They must learn that once we have collected our jumbled thoughts, our writing must be structured first into sentences, then into paragraphs by grouping together sentences about the same aspect of our topic. Paragraph structure must be taught and children need examples of how ideas can be grouped together by topic and that a change of idea means a change of paragraph.

Demonstrate by doing

It is important to further develop the environment of **shared** and **guided writing** begun at sentence level, i.e. composing together, demonstrating how to select information, and to organize it in paragraphs. Use such opportunities to talk through more complex paragraph structure and punctuation skills. Demonstrate how to combine sentences to create variety and cohesion. Show the children ways of linking paragraphs using suitable connectives. Consider the use of **writing frames** for organizing longer pieces of writing. Explicitly teach the use of exclamation marks, question marks, and inverted commas, so that children appreciate how they help the reader to understand what we have written.

As the children's capabilities develop, instruction will be less invasive and the emphasis will be on them becoming independent writers. Whilst the children need your help to master the writing process, point out that creativity only really begins when they express their own ideas. In this way the children will feel empowered to write.

Styles of writing

Children need plenty of opportunity for independent practice, writing across a range of **genres** on topics that interest them. These can take numerous forms: narration/stories, descriptions, letters, instructions, informational writing, research reports, and **persuasive writing**.

Descriptions feature in 5.1, which uses the famous painting *Van Gogh's bedroom* beginning with a description of the painting, then asking children to write about their own bedroom. Older children could write a comparison with their bedroom. Descriptions also feature in 5.13, 'Music as a stimulus for descriptive writing', where the teacher describes scenes conjured up by the music, and the children write what they visualize. Some children may tell whole stories, others may just describe a feeling or place, but practice with different kinds of music could lead to more extended descriptive writing.

Sequencing a recipe in 5.3, 'Jumbled recipes', focuses on the importance of writing instructions in the right order. The children are invited to create their own recipes and submit them to the book's website.

Though very different in nature, 5.4, 'Surveys', and 5.6, 'When my grandparents went to school', both involve conducting a survey and writing up the findings. Both have personal relevance and practise factual reporting.

Persuasive writing is a challenge for children, so 5.5, 'Top celebrity', combines an interest in celebrities, such as popstars and sports personalities, with researching them. Using the research findings, children must try to persuade others that their chosen celebrity is the best in their field. The challenge is to persuade others to attend the next performance of the star by exchanging letters.

5.7, 'Creating a greetings mat', focuses on letter writing and is supported by the creation of a mat with writing prompts, a kind of text bank, so that the children have a resource for future use. This is practised in 5.8, 'Post-it memos', which is about party invitations and replies.

Narrative is the focus of the next four activities. 5.9, 'Comic strip stories', consists of sequencing and telling a story in comic strips. 5.10, 'Putting myself in the picture', is a personal story with the child as the central character and includes a homemade book. 5.11, 'Mini stories', is a group story inspired by pictures to help children to compose mini stories. 5.12, 'Win-a-word stories', is another group story, in which teams have basic words for their story but have the opportunity to win extra words to enhance their writing.

A note on writing stories

If you have been using stories in class, the children will have a sense of what an English text looks like and be familiar with how stories are structured. Emphasize what makes a good story by pointing out specific parts of the narrative structure such as setting, character, plot, solution, and ending. You should also consider the language of beginnings and endings. When children begin to create stories of their own, they will see that they are copying real authors.

Presentation

Drafting and redrafting can be tedious and many children prefer to skip it. Explain that with a little extra care they will be able to feel very proud of their writing. Editing with children is best led by you, challenging them to think about what they have written, for example, through questioning: *Does this make sense? Who said this? Should there be speech marks? Is it a question? How do we show that in writing? Can you think of a way of joining these two short sentences? Are all the similar ideas grouped together?* Encourage the use of word banks, word walls, and dictionaries to encourage children to check for accuracy.

By the time children have reached final draft stage, the emphasis is on presentation and accuracy. Encourage them to do a best copy. They could make the page attractive by using colour, underlining, and spacing. If they use a word processor, get them to look at the spacing and layout on preview before printing.

Be unpredictable

Whilst children like routine, avoid always using the same approach to writing. Be a little inventive sometimes! Try playing music as they write, let the children choose the topic from time to time, put a story frame on the board or overhead projector and have the children work from that. Take advantage of graphic organizers to download and give them different formats for similar tasks. If they usually write in an exercise book, give them coloured paper or shaped paper to write on occasionally.

At the end of this stage, clearly some children will be further along the path to **independent writing** than others, yet with encouragement and support the majority of children will be able to write using a variety of strategies in a number of different **genres**, and be able to communicate as confident, capable writers.

Descriptions

5.1 Van Gogh's bedroom

LEVEL	2+
AGE	8+
TIME	30 minutes
AIMS	**To help children to write simple texts about their bedroom or another room in their house; to look at a work of art and write about it.**
PREPARATION	Find or download a reproduction of one of Van Gogh's paintings of his bedroom (see Further Reading for web addresses). Find out how much it is worth now in local currency.

Van Gogh's Bedroom at Arles (1889). Musée d'Orsay, Paris.

IN CLASS

1 Show the children the Van Gogh picture. Tell them that the artist was called Vincent Van Gogh and although he is very famous now, he was very poor when he was alive. Tell them how much this painting is worth now.

2 Elicit the vocabulary they can see: *window, chairs, bed, pictures, mirror, table, walls, floor.* You could also teach *blanket, sheets, pillows, coat hook,* if they are useful words for your class.

3 Draw a table on the board similar to the one below and write in the nouns in column 5.

1	2	3	4	5
				chair
				window
				pictures
				bed
				blanket
				walls

4 Elicit the colours they can see in the painting and encourage them to make pairs with the nouns, for example, *blue walls*, *a red blanket*, and write the colours in column 4 next to the correct noun.

5 Remind the children that when we want to describe the existence of something, we can say: *There is (there's)/There are*. Write *There* in column 1 and *is/are* in column 2.

6 Add *a/an* in column 3 if the noun is singular or *some* if it is plural. Alternatively, you may wish to add numbers in this column, for example, *There are two brown chairs*.

7 Now ask the children to think of their own bedroom and to write sentences about it, referring to the table above.

VARIATION 1

You could add another column before the colours and elicit other adjectives to describe the furniture, for example, *big*, *small*, *pretty*, and encourage the children to follow this model when writing about their own room. Teach or revise prepositions so that they can write a more detailed description of Van Gogh's bedroom or their own room, for example, *There is a table and chair in front of the window*.

VARIATION 2

Children could make their own version of Van Gogh's room by colouring the page on the Enchanted Learning website (see Further Reading).

They then write about their picture following the pattern of the table.

FOLLOW-UP 1

Children with a higher level of English could compare their bedroom with Van Gogh's: *Van Gogh's bedroom is bigger than my room. There's a computer and TV in my room. Van Gogh has got two chairs and I've got one. I prefer my bedroom because... I think it looks comfortable because...*

FOLLOW-UP 2

The children can send email postcards of Van Gogh's paintings from the electronic postcard websites in Further Reading.

5.2 Funny dictations

LEVEL	2+
AGE	7+
TIME	20 minutes +
AIMS	**To prepare the children for writing texts about themselves; to interview and write about others.**
PREPARATION	Create your own gap-fill exercise or use the one in Worksheet 5.2. Make a copy for each child.

IN CLASS

1 Tell the children to write the numbers 1–14 down the page and then tell them what they need to write, for example, in Worksheet 5.2:

> *Number one is a person's name.*
> *Number two is the name of a place.*
> *Number three is a year, for example, 19_, 20_.*
> *Number four is a man's name.*
> *Number five is a job.*
> *Number six is a woman's name.*
> *Number seven is a job.*
> *Number eight is a colour.*
> *Number nine is a colour.*
> *Number ten is a number.*
> *Number eleven is a number.*
> *Number twelve is an adjective to describe people.*
> *Number thirteen is an animal.*
> *Number fourteen is a name.*

2 Now give each child a copy of the Worksheet. They write their words in the spaces in the text.

3 Once they have finished, they read their text and then exchange it with other children.

COMMENTS

This is usually humorous as the children have to write the words before seeing the text and they tend to choose words they like, so they may end up with a text like the following:

> My father, Brad Pitt, is a policeman and my mother, Julia Roberts, is an electrician. I've got pink eyes and blue hair. I have ten brothers and four sisters. They are all very small. I have a pet hippo called Dolores.

FOLLOW-UP

The children write a paragraph about themselves using the same model. Collect the texts and read out the information, omitting the child's name. The class try to guess who you are reading about.

5.3   Jumbled recipes

LEVEL	2 +
AGE	8+
TIME	40 minutes
AIMS	**To model the language of giving instructions so that the children can follow them and write instructions for others.**
MATERIALS	A recipe (see 3.6, 'Making milkshakes', in Sarah Phillips' *Young Learners* in this series), pencils, paper, coloured paper, glue, something to stick the recipes to the wall.
PREPARATION	Type or write out the recipe so that each step is on a separate line. Make a copy for each group. Cut up the recipes line by line, and mix up the lines. Attach the jumbled recipes to the wall and fix a piece of coloured paper above each one so that the groups know which is theirs.

IN CLASS

1 Divide the class into groups of three and assign each group a colour.

2 Follow the rules for 4.8, 'Running dictation'. Choose one child as the writer and the other two as runners.

3 Explain that each group has a recipe but that the steps are mixed up. Each group must dictate the steps of the recipe to each other so that they can put them in the right order.

4 In turns, the runners go and read their recipe, come back, and dictate a step to the writer.

5 Once they have finished, they read the recipe together and put the steps in the correct order.

6 Allow them to make their recipes more attractive by creating decorative borders, or a shape such as a fancy milkshake glass for their writing.

The Scrummy Sandwich

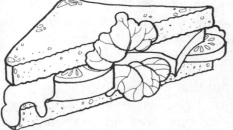

2 slices bread
butter
lettuce
tomatoes
cheese slices
cucumber
mayonnaise
butter bread, layer salad
and cheese add mayonnaise

granary bread
butter
lettuce
tomatoes
cucumber
cheese slices
mayonnaise

VARIATION	The children can then use the language to create their own recipes. Encourage them to design a healthy recipe, for example, a healthy sandwich or fruit salad and brainstorm the ingredients, writing them on the board. The children then decide on the recipe before writing out the instructions, following the model of the Jumbled Recipe. They could email their recipes to this book's website (see back cover for web address), where the best entries will be displayed.

5.4   Surveys

LEVEL	2+
AGE	8+
TIME	**30-40 minutes**
AIMS	**To formulate questions and use them to find out information.**
PREPARATION	1 In a previous lesson, brainstorm ideas for topics the children would like to interview their classmates about and write them on the board for the class to decide on one (for example, hobbies).
	2 Prepare a questionnaire or use Worksheet 5.4. Make a copy for each child.
IN CLASS	1 Tell the children they are going to do a survey of their class.
	2 Give out the questionnaire and show them how to formulate questions. For example:
	Find someone who plays sport (which?) → *Do you play a sport? Which sport do you play?*
	3 Ask each child to come out in turn and write their questions on the board. Practise the questions with the children.
	4 Tell the children that they have to find just one person who can answer each question and fill in that person's name.
	5 The children circulate and ask the questions. Once they have finished, they sit down and review their answers. Ask for verbal feedback and write details on the board, for example, if anyone has unusual hobbies, won awards for their hobby, etc. The nice thing about this type of questionnaire is that the children have different answers.
	6 The children then write up their findings. You could let them decide what they focus on, for example, a general report or specific hobbies.
	7 To complete their task they may wish to ask some children for more information about their hobby.

FOLLOW-UP   Design a writing frame for the children to write up their findings. Give them the beginnings of sentences or gap fills for them to complete, for example:

> *Most children said … Some children … Only … said … Hardly any children … A few children … Out of … children, only …*

COMMENTS   We have used 'Find someone who … ' as it involves the children formulating questions first. You can use a different format if you wish.

5.5 Top celebrity

LEVEL   3+

AGE   10+

TIME   40 minutes

AIMS   **To use reading skills to research information about a famous person; to transfer knowledge from reading into writing; to write a letter or series of letters to persuade others to change their minds.**

MATERIALS   Interviews of famous people, videoed or printed and displayed with photographs according to the resources available.

PREPARATION   Look through popular magazines and newspapers, and video TV interviews with famous people the children know. Do an Internet search if you have access, as most famous personalities have websites dedicated to them.

IN CLASS   1 Put the children in groups of three and ask each group to choose a celebrity to research.

2 The groups identify four or five questions they want to find the answers to, for example, the person's likes or dislikes, their background, childhood, family, future wishes, or a typical day. Revise the question forms if necessary. Monitor and check the questions.

3 The children look through the materials you have prepared and try to answer their questions. If not, they can suggest other sources they may know or search the Internet if they have access (see *The Internet and Young Learners*, in this series).

4 The children review their answers. If there are any gaps, encourage the children to suggest possible answers by asking questions such as: *What type of diet and exercise must a top footballer have to stay fit? What is the daily training routine of an Olympic athlete?*

5 Encourage the groups to ask each other questions, as other members of the class may know some of the answers.

6 Go round monitoring the children's progress, suggesting how they could make their text more interesting, for example, does their celebrity have a fear of anything? Do they have an unusual hobby?

7 Decide on, or allow the children to choose, a method of presenting the information, for example:
   a A magazine format with pictures and short pieces of text. Collect the reports in a class magazine.
   b A poster with pictures and text. Display the posters and allow the children time to go round reading one another's. You could then use the information to ask the children questions about the celebrities.

8 The letter writing is best done as individuals or in pairs. The children must make the case that their celebrity is the best in their field, for example, best footballer. In order to do this, they write a letter to persuade another child to accompany them to the star's next performance. This works well if fans of rival stars try to persuade each other. The class judges who makes the best case.

FOLLOW-UP

Most celebrities have fan clubs and the children could find the address on the Internet (they need to make sure it is the official site) and write a letter or an email to the person.

5.6 When my grandparents went to school

LEVEL

3+

AGE

9+

TIME

30 minutes plus an extra 20 minutes for pre-class task

AIMS

To create interview questions in the simple past tense; to use information from an interview with a family member; to write a text in English.

MATERIALS

Information about school life in the past, for example, unusual objects, old exercise books, or school photographs.

PREPARATION

Tell the children that they are going to interview an older family member about what school was like when they were young. They should prepare by asking them if they have any special memories and whether they would be prepared to lend photographs, certificates, etc.

IN CLASS

1 Ask the children what kinds of similarities and differences they think there are between school now and in the past. Write on the board things they would like to know about those times, for example, school age, classrooms, subjects, uniforms, friends, punishments, teachers, buildings, sports, homework, exams.

2 Revise question forms and ask the children to suggest the questions they need to ask their relatives. Write suitable questions on the board, for example:

How old were you when you started school? Did you wear a uniform? What subjects did you study? Were the teachers strict? What was the classroom like?

3 The children copy the questions they wish to ask. Then they interview their relatives. They can use the English questions as prompts although they will need to do the interview in their mother tongue. They record the responses.

4 Back in class translate the answers and map out the text with the children. You may need to revise ways of writing about the past. You could give them a frame with some sentences to finish so that they end up with a complete text, for example:

> I interviewed my …
> His/her name is …
> When he/she was young, he/she (go) …
> He/she (learn) … every day.
> Once a week/fortnight/month they went …
> He/she studied …
> They did/didn't (wear) a uniform.
> The teachers were …
> The subject he/she (like) best/least was …
> His/her special memory of school is ………………
> He/she also (go) … the cinema/theatre/ice-skating every week.

Photocopiable © Oxford University Press

5 Once the children have finished, help them edit their work.

6 They write out or word-process their text and attach a photo if they have one.

7 Display the work and let the children go round reading one another's.

FOLLOW-UP

You could make this into an ongoing project. The children choose other topics to find out about, for example, what people's diet was like—was it healthier than now? They may ask about an object from the past, for example, something which is not widely used now, such as a game or household object. The children could find out what it is, who would use it, when, and what for?

| **VARIATION 1** | Children interview their parents about their jobs, or older siblings about secondary school, and then write the interview up. |

| **VARIATION 2** | The children interview family members about their village/town/city. They make a brochure for families coming on holiday to the area. |

Letters

5.7 Creating a greetings mat—a text bank

| **LEVEL** | 2+ |

| **AGE** | 6+ |

| **TIME** | 30 minutes + |

| **AIMS** | **To create text banks which the children can refer to when writing greetings cards or letters; to make the children more independent learners in class.** |

| **MATERIALS** | Some coloured card or paper if laminating, coloured pencils or fine felt pens, coloured card, a folder to keep the text mats where the children can access them easily. |

| **PREPARATION** | Prepare an example greetings mat, for instance about birthdays, which includes some short texts for which children might need to write a thank-you card or letter. |

Write the texts in different colours on a piece of coloured card and decorate the card. Now put it inside a plastic sleeve or laminate to keep it clean when the children take it to their table to copy from.

IN CLASS

1   Show the children your sample greetings mat and read out some of the texts. Ask the children when you would write these types of messages.

2   Try and elicit some more messages by asking the children when you would thank someone, for example, for an invitation, for a gift, or for help.

3   Ask the children about other times they might write to people and to whom, for example, at Christmas—sending cards to grandma/grandpa, cousins, friends, a letter to Father Christmas (or whoever brings their presents, the Three Kings, the baby Jesus, etc.); Chinese New Year—thanking the family for their red packets; Eid or Diwali messages; or invitations to parties.

4   Elicit ways of starting the message: *Dear, To, Hi, Hello*.

5   Divide the children into groups of three or four. Tell them that they are going to make a mat in their group which you are going to put in a plastic sleeve for them to look at when they want to write a letter.

6   Let them choose the purpose for their greetings mat (see step 3).

7   The children plan their texts with pencil and paper. You will need to monitor and assist.

8   It is very important that the mats have correct spellings because others may copy their mistakes.

9   Once the children have finished, they decorate their greetings mats and put them in a plastic sleeve in a folder. Use file dividers to sort the greetings mats by topic.

5.8   Post-it memos

LEVEL	3+
AGE	8+
TIME	**10 minutes in the first lesson, 20 minutes in the second lesson**
AIMS	**To take brief notes and develop them into a text; to write an email.**
MATERIALS	Small pieces of paper, preferably sticky (for example, 'Post-it' notes).
PREPARATION	Prepare some information about an event, for example, a party, and write it on to the pieces of paper. (See the example below.)

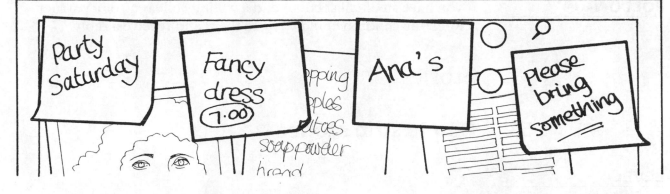

IN CLASS

Lesson 1

1 Tell the children that your brother or sister took a telephone message for you about a party and has written the information on a note but it is not very clear and you need their help to work out the exact details of the party.

2 Stick the notes to the board and read out the information. Write the information in bigger letters so all the children can see.

3 Work through the information, trying to fill in any gaps. Elicit the questions you need to ask. Which Saturday? Which Ana?—you know several Anas. Where is the party? What does she want me to bring? Is there a theme for the fancy dress?

4 Tell the children you will need to phone your friend and to find out more information.

Lesson 2

1 Start from step 1 again, as in lesson 1.

2 Add the missing information: Saturday and a date, Ana + surname, address, a cake.

3 Tell them you need to send a letter or an email to your friend to say thank you for the invitation and that you will be going to the party. Ask how you might start it, reminding the children that you are writing to a friend. You may use *Dear Ana*, but you could use *Hello* or *Hi*.

4 Establish that next you need to say why you are emailing, for example, *Thank you for inviting me to the party*. You need to confirm you will be going, the time, date and place, and what you will bring. Model the format on the board and elicit the information from the children. For example:

I will see you on (elicit the day and date) *at* (elicit the time) *at* (elicit the venue). Then elicit the information about what you will take: *I'll bring a cake* (elicit the type of cake you might take).

5 Now divide the children into groups. Give them notes with information about another event. The children draft a letter or an email to send to the person. They may have to include questions if there is some information missing, for example, what time they should meet.

FOLLOW-UP   If you have an email account and a willing colleague or a partner school, the children could write to them and receive a reply.

Stories

5.9 Comic strip stories

LEVEL   2+

AGE   7+

TIME   **20–30 minutes**

AIMS   **To reinforce knowledge of the narrative structure of stories; to describe action pictures; to practise sequencing skills; to give the opportunity to write English as it is spoken.**

MATERIALS   A comic strip, for example, from a magazine or newspaper: an enlarged version for you and a normal size one for each group of four or five children.

PREPARATION

1 Select a comic strip and delete the dialogue. Then photocopy and enlarge it and cut it into frames. (Alternatively, photocopy it on to a transparency and cut it into frames.)

2 Photocopy, for each group of children, the same comic strip and cut it into frames. Place each set in an envelope.

IN CLASS

1 Place the large comic strip on the board or overhead projector in random order. Ask the children what is happening in each picture.

2 Ask: *Which picture is at the beginning of the story? What happens next? What happens after that?*

3 Invite individual children to come and place them in order, leaving space for you to draw large speech bubbles on the board coming from the mouths of the characters.

4 Elicit what the children think the characters might be saying. Write the dialogue in large letters in the speech bubbles.

5 Show how you can write extra detail, such as where the action is taking place, in text boxes at the top or bottom of the pictures.

6 Put the children in groups and give out the envelopes.

7 Tell the children to arrange the pictures into a possible story order. Monitor their progress, helping with the order sequence and dialogue.

8 When everyone in the group is happy with the order of the pictures, they glue their comic strip on to a piece of paper. They then draw speech bubbles and write in the dialogue and any other details.

9 Display the work and allow each group to read out their version.

10 Collect them into a class comic book.

5.10 Putting myself in the picture

The children publish a book, going through all the stages of composing the story, drafting and planning, designing, illustrating, and making the book. The book is designed with a cut-out of themselves so that they feature on each page of the story as the pages are turned over.

LEVEL	2+
AGE	8+
TIME	**60–90 minutes (can be a project over several lessons)**
AIMS	**To write a story with a narrative structure, i.e. beginning, middle, and end; to use pictures and words to organize a text; to design a storyboard.**
MATERIALS	A diagram to illustrate the narrative structure; card for the front cover, paper, rulers, scissors, glue, stapler, pens, and pencils.

PREPARATION

1 Draw a representation of the narrative structure on the board or on a poster, like a piece of cake with three layers (see the illustration on the next page).

2 Make a sample book to show the children.

IN CLASS

1 Show the children your book and explain that they are going to write a story in which they are the main character. Explain that it can be a true story or fictional. Demonstrate how the figure can be placed in the frame for each part of the story.

2 Show the children the plan of a story, using your diagram. Tell them that each layer of the cake is important, but the most delicious cakes are those with tasty fillings. If the middle of the story is boring, the reader will be bored.

3 Ask the children to think of things that could happen to them. Start to build up a story map with sketches and words on the board.

4 Help the children to draft an outline of their stories. Give them some paper and ask questions like: *What happened to you? Where were you? When? How old were you? How did you feel? Was anyone else there? Who? What did they say? What did they do? What happened next? How did it end?*

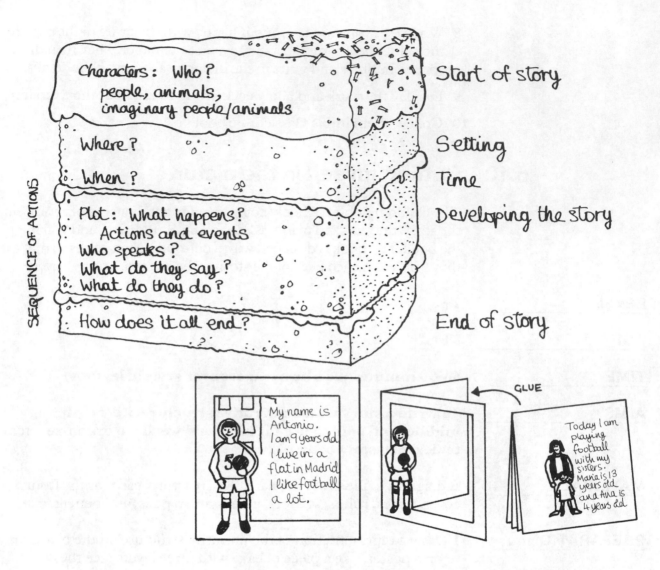

5 Once they have an outline, they can sketch a story map with words and pictures. Make sure they realize that they do not draw themselves in any of the pictures because they are that character on the front.

6 Put the children in groups and get them to describe the story to the other children. The others should give comments and advice: Does it follow logical steps? Can they understand it? Could it be more exciting? Circulate and monitor. The children decide whether to take the advice and make changes.

7 When you and they are satisfied with the draft, they are ready to design their book. They need to sketch out the pages in order to know how many they need.

8 They make the final draft of the story and illustrations, making sure that the main part of the action is visible through the window of the cover.

9 Lastly, they make a drawing of themselves, cut it out and stick it on to a folded piece of card so that it stands out. As the pages of the inner book are turned, the figure can be positioned to fit in each frame.

5.11 Mini stories

These are very short stories, which are easily completed in one lesson and involve the children working together in pairs or groups to write and edit a complete story. Each story must have a beginning, a middle, and an end.

LEVEL	2+
AGE	8+
TIME	20–30 minutes
AIMS	**To generate ideas for stories from pictures; to work with others to create a story; to focus on the narrative structure of beginning, middle, and end.**
MATERIALS	Two sets of two or three pictures with people and scenes that could be linked to make a story. You need one set of pictures large enough for you to model the activity from the front, and another set to photocopy for the children, scrap paper, and marker pens.
PREPARATION	Cut out the pictures. Prepare your example and enlarge it if necessary. Photocopy the other pictures, one set for each group.
IN CLASS	

1 Attach your set of pictures to the board. Tell the children they are going to help you to write a very short story about what they see in the pictures.

2 Encourage the children to compose a sentence or two about each picture. Starting with the first picture, elicit information by asking questions like: *Who can you see in the picture? How old are they? What do they look like? What are they wearing? Are they friends? Mother and son? Brother and sister? What are they doing? What are they saying?* Also ask questions to do with the rules of writing, such as *How do I write the first letter in the sentence? What comes at the end of a sentence? How do I show that this is the name of a place?* Write the suggestions on the board.

3 Next, explore the location: *Where is this? Town? City? Which country?* Ask the children to decide: *How did they get to this place? What happens next? Where will they go?*

4 Finally, explore possible endings: *How does the story end?*

5 Ask the children to read the story sentence by sentence. Ask if they want to make any changes. Explain that this very short story has everything a long story has: a beginning, a problem to solve, an answer to the problem, and an ending.

6 Put the children in groups and give out the sets of pictures. Tell the children to arrange the pictures in any order and decide on the plot of a story by looking carefully and asking themselves questions about them.

7 Give out paper and markers. Let the children take turns to write the group story, or choose a 'secretary' for each group.

COMMENTS

If the children can work on a computer, it will be easier for them to edit their stories.

5.12   Win-a-word stories

LEVEL

3+

AGE

7+

TIME

40 minutes

AIMS

To learn vocabulary for a story.

PREPARATION

Choose a subject for a story, for example, 'holidays'. Write a list of about 20 questions (these can be general knowledge or language-based) and give each question a number. Don't show the children.

IN CLASS

1 Brainstorm vocabulary the children might need for this kind of story, for example, if the topic is *holidays*, they might choose: *beach, swimming, sandcastles, picnic, lemonade, ice cream*. The children copy the words into their books.

2 Divide the class into groups of three or four.

3 Each group takes it in turns to give you a number. Ask them the question with that number from the list you prepared earlier.

4 If they get it right, they can choose a word for their story. If they cannot answer the question, or get it wrong, allow one of the other groups to answer and choose the word they want for their story.

5 The first group to win five words is the winner. When one group has won five words, give the other groups words to make five.

6 The groups must write a story which includes their five words but none of the other groups' five words.

5.13   Music as a stimulus for descriptive writing

LEVEL	3+
AGE	8+
TIME	30 minutes
AIMS	**To use listening skills; to visualize places and events when listening to music.**
PREPARATION	Listen to various types of music and select those you feel the children would enjoy and which also evoke strong impressions of place and atmosphere.

IN CLASS

1 Tell the children that you are going to play some music and that they should close their eyes and imagine a place.

2 Play the music and ask the children:

–What can you see?   *–What time of year is it?*
–What are the colours?   *–Who is with you?*
–What sounds do you hear?   *–Who is talking?*
–What are you doing?   *–What are they saying?*
–What are you wearing?   *–How do you feel?*
–What time of day is it?   *–What is happening?*

3 Play it again, and, as the music comes to an end, ask the children to take a last careful look at this special place, noticing all the details.

4 The children make a list of what they saw and then write a description.

VARIATION

Less experienced writers may work better in pairs. They could produce a shared piece of writing or write up individual versions of jointly prepared writing.

COMMENTS

The idea of this activity is to encourage the children, through listening to music, to think about an imaginary place and things which may happen there. Depending on the age of the children and the music, this can lead to a number of different places and far beyond the classroom. Younger children may write, not about an imagined place, but about somewhere they know well, such as the park or the beach.

FOLLOW-UP

See 6.9, 'Musical daydreaming'.

6 Poetry

Children get so much pleasure from songs, poems, rhythm, rhymes, and chants that it seems natural there should be a section on poetry in a book about children's writing. We need to tap into different ways for children to express themselves and poetry may add a new dimension to your writing curriculum. Having a different format could encourage new abilities and may even lead to an enduring love of poetry.

Why write poetry?

Children pick up songs, poems, rhymes, rhythms, and playground chants very easily and they are a good way to demonstrate how we can be creative with English words. Through poetry, the children learn in an unconscious way the skills of writing descriptively, and the use of features like **alliteration**, **rhyme**, **metaphor**, **imagery**, and **simile**.

Poetry may appeal to those children who find writing prose difficult and give them an opportunity to achieve. Since poems are shorter than stories, it is easier for children to practise the process of drafting and refining to produce a finished piece of writing.

Learning by listening

In our experience children enjoy listening to poetry and it can motivate them to write their own. As you read they can hear the rhythm in the pattern of the words, and also how individual words can have an auditory impact, especially alliterative and rhyming words. They learn that not all poems rhyme, but children like those that do because they are fun to listen to.

Choosing poems

As children are unable to understand deep or hidden meanings, we need poems which appeal to children and can motivate them to express themselves in similar ways. Children's poems are included in some activities and an Internet search will find websites with poems both for and by children; some even have recordings to listen to.

Whether you read the work of published poets or children, choose poems you like and can enjoy with the children. Listening to poetry gives children the pleasure of engaging with other writers so that when they write they will feel like real poets.

This unit is designed to be used a little like a road map through this particular genre; you can choose to visit one or two places or you can take the whole tour. The ideas featured are just a few possibilities, but they should help to encourage creativity.

Continued support

Earlier recommendations for **shared writing** apply to writing poetry. At first the children will need lots of guidance and that is why the unit begins at word level with acronyms and list poems. Even very reluctant writers will produce a word list from a brainstorming session and many will be able to develop it much further. Elicited lists from other activities become a class resource for composing poems like these. You could even create special lists for poetry sessions, for example, alliterative words and words which rhyme.

Poetry lends itself to illustration, and shape poems (see 6.5, 'Shape poems') at sentence level, which follow the outline of something, are especially appealing to children. Poems with a limited number of words (see 6.4 'Lantern poems') and variations such as **haiku** and **cinquains** are particularly suited to EFL learners.

Children also need to learn to write in verse so will benefit from shared writing activities like 6.6, 'I like/I don't like', which uses this structure (*I like/don't like*) to create a poem and has a repetitive rhythm. The Variation is an idea using *I can/can't* which addresses issues of self-esteem and feelings, allowing children to reflect on their strong points.

The poems in 6.7, 'Poems based on the senses', are written to a model or format. Far from stifling creativity, writing to a format almost guarantees success and operates with equal success at different levels depending on the age of the children.

Music is the inspiration for poetry in 6.9, 'Musical daydreaming', and although it is structured by the teacher's talkover, the children are free to choose the scene and events, allowing them to write either factually about familiar places and people or about entirely imaginary ones. The children could word-process their poems, following the example in 3.8, 'Pictograms'.

For more ideas on writing poems, see Jane Spiro's *Creative Poetry Writing* in the Resource Books for Teachers series. Although aimed mainly at older learners, some activities can be used with children.

Ideas for publication

Exploit any means of publication available to make the children's work special:

– create class anthologies to keep in the library or book corner
– allow the children to copy poems on to decorated paper for display. Encourage them to be inventive, for example, poems about music written on a CD case; poems about rain on a raindrop shape suspended from the ceiling
– download some interesting fonts for them to word-process poems for display or to add to a class anthology; allow the children to choose the font and to print in colour
– import images from the Internet to illustrate their poems
– utilize multi-media to enhance their creativity, for example, older children could do a PowerPoint version with animation and downloaded video clips
– allow the children to record themselves reading the poems
– if possible, share the poems with another class at a poetry-reading session
– publish their work on poetry websites, a school website, classroom or school display board
– the children could write out their poems with pictograms or use other techniques from activity 3.8, 'Pictograms', such as word-processing using different fonts to depict words as in Variation 4
– if there is a national poetry day, the children could write some English poems.

You can send your children's poems to this book's website: www.oup.com/elt/teacher/rbt. Children and teachers whose poems are displayed will receive free books.

Word level

6.1 Acrostics

LEVEL	1+
AGE	8+
TIME	20–30 minutes
AIMS	**To create simple word patterns from known words; to create a piece of writing which is meaningful to the children.**
PREPARATION	Prepare examples of acrostics with vocabulary familiar to the children.

IN CLASS

1 Choose a name or word. Write the letters vertically and think of words which begin with each letter to describe the topic, for example:

Child's example using her mother's name	An example using the word 'friends'
Mummy	**F**orever
Architect	**R**osa
Running	**I**ce-cream
Italian	**E**leven
Always happy	**N**ice
By Ilaria, aged 10	**D**ancing
	Special
	By Begoña, aged 11

2 Show the children the sample acrostics, and explain the significance of the words chosen. In the second example above, Begoña's best friend is called Rosa, she likes ice-cream, she's 11, Rosa is a nice person, they go dancing together, Rosa is a very special person.

3 Let the children try writing an acrostic using their name or a word. Children with long names may prefer to use a nickname or to choose a word they like.

4 Once they have drafted their acrostic, ask them to write it out neatly and decorate it. It is a good idea for them to do the initial letters in a different colour so that the acrostic word stands out.

VARIATION

With older children you can use an acrostic to revise vocabulary from a topic in a coursebook, for example, words about the environment:

Greenhouse effect
Acid rain
Rubbish
Bin
Atmosphere
Global warming
Earth

By Dani, aged 12

6.2 List poems

LEVEL   1+

AGE   8+

TIME   20–30 minutes

AIMS   **To listen to poems and write their own versions; to use topic-based vocabulary creatively.**

PREPARATION

1 Check there are enough appropriate words in the word banks (see activity 3.1).

2 Write or choose an example of a poem.

IN CLASS

1 Choose a topic, for example, 'food', and brainstorm all the vocabulary the children know on this topic: nouns, verbs, and adjectives. If you have word banks, refer the children to them. Write all the words on the board.

2 Tell the children you are going to read a poem, the title of the poem, and the name and age of the author. It is a good idea to use a poem written by another child like this example:

> **My favourite pizza**
> Ham,
> Cheese,
> Tomato,
> Pineapple,
> And
> Sausage.
> My favourite pizza.
> **Mmm! Delicious!**
>
> By Manuela, aged 8

3 Ask what they like on their favourite pizzas. Write the vocabulary on the board.

4 Get them to make a list of toppings. It is a good idea to give them the title and last line (written in bold in the example).

5 The children could create pictures, writing their poems in a circle and drawing their pizza in the middle.

VARIATION 1

With more advanced children, elicit adjectives to describe colours and tastes or textures, for example, *juicy red tomatoes*, *delicious ham*, or *sweet pineapple*.

VARIATION 2

1 Provide the children with a title, for example, a recipe and some sentence starters:

> **How to make my favourite sandwich:**
> First the bread,
> Then the ....,
> ....,
> ....,
> ....
> More bread to finish.
> GREAT!

2 The children make a poster, and draw and colour each layer of the poem like a many-layered sandwich.

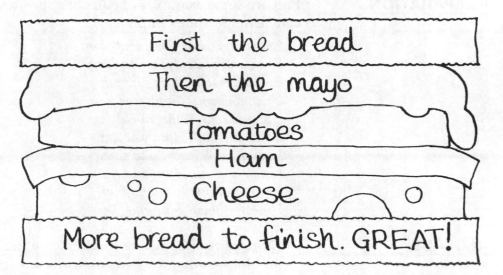

VARIATION 3

Elicit combinations of foods they like to eat together, for example:

> Bread and honey
> Ice-cream and chocolate sauce
> Cheese and tomatoes
> Chicken and gravy
> Fried fish and ketchup
> Eggs with chips
> These are all my favourite foods
> When I can choose what I have for tea.

VARIATION 4

Ask the children to write lists limited to three or four words on a theme, for example, school friends. Three words about: the school, friends' names, special personal qualities, favourite lessons, sports they play, food they like, games they play, things they find funny, things they are good at, why we like them.

VARIATION 5

Choose a letter to practise **alliteration** and make lists of words beginning with this letter. Add other words with the same sound in them.

6.3   Opposites and rhyming words poem

LEVEL	2+
AGE	8+
TIME	20 minutes
AIMS	To practise opposites; to collect rhymes; to use knowledge of rhyme and rime for creative writing (see Chapter 3, 'Word level'); to explore sound patterns in words; to reinforce spelling.
PREPARATION	Prepare some examples of pairs of opposites from which rhymes can be made, for example:

> *Black and white, Day and night*
> *Read and write, Heavy or light*
> *Big and small, Short and tall*
> *Up and down, Country or town*
> *Hot and cold, Young or old*
> *Good and bad, Happy or sad*
> *In and out, Whisper and shout*
> *Listen and talk, Run and walk*
> *Earth and sky, Low and high*
> *Hide and show, Fast and slow*

IN CLASS

1 Write pairs of opposites randomly on the board. Demonstrate to the children that the pairs of words are opposites and that some of the pairs rhyme.

2 See if the children can match the rhyming pairs of opposites and ask them to come and draw an arrow between them.

3 Try to elicit more rhyming opposites.

4 Ask the children to put some pairs of opposites together to make a poem.

FOLLOW-UP

The children could make pictograms of rhyming pairs (see 3.8, 'Pictograms', and 3.18, 'Sounds the same, looks different').

6.4 Lantern poems

Poems written in a plan of five lines and counted syllables per line. This makes the shape of a lantern.

LEVEL	**3+**
AGE	**8+**
TIME	**30 minutes**
AIMS	**To write a poem using a fixed number of syllables; to explore syllables in English words; to design shapes with words.**
MATERIALS	Some visual impetus to inspire the children, for example, a sparkling ring, a piece of pottery or a patterned ceramic tile, or natural materials such as pine cones, a rose, or an item of clothing such as a wedding dress or large hat.

PREPARATION

1 Choose a special object to show the children and think of words the children know to describe it.

2 Make an example lantern poem large enough for the class to see, using these guidelines:

   Line 1: One syllable
   Line 2: Two syllables
   Line 3: Three syllables
   Line 4: Three/four syllables
   Line 5: One syllable.

IN CLASS

1 Read your model poem to the children and explain the meaning.

2 Explain what syllables are (see the Glossary and 3.7, 'Clapping games').

3 Read the poem two or three times, encouraging the children to say the words and clap out the syllables.

4 Show the children an object you want them to create a poem about and elicit words to describe it.

5 Write them in random order at the sides of the board.

6 Draw four columns on the board and number them one to four.

7 Read out the words and sort them into columns according to the number of syllables.

8 Now ask the children to work in groups, using words from the board to make a lantern shape poem.

Example 1   For younger children

Ball
Bouncy
Yellow and blue.
Big and round
Play!

Example 2   For older children

TV
Funny
Interesting
Cartoon time.
Great!

Example 3   For older, more advanced children

Shells.
Listen!
Hear the sounds.
Waves on the beach
Ssswoosh!

VARIATION 1

Cinquains

A cinquain is a five-line poem. This type of poem works best about a noun which appears in the title—poems about abstract things are not so successful. There is a pattern of 22 syllables to the verse, as follows:

Line 1: noun—usually 2 syllables
Line 2: describes the noun—usually 4 syllables
Line 3: states action—usually 6 syllables
Line 4: expresses a feeling—usually 8 syllables
Line 5: synonym of line 1—usually 2 or 3 syllables

Example

'Pizza'
Pizza!
I like pizza.
Where is it now?
In the cook's hands.
Where is it now?
Yum! Yum!

By Xi Mengyuan, aged 11

VARIATION 2	**Haiku**

Haiku is a traditional Japanese poetry form which lends itself to English language teaching. Choose objects or pictures which encourage the children to write, for example, Van Gogh's painting *Sunflowers*. A haiku consists of three lines and there should be a total of 17 syllables as follows:

Line 1: 5 syllables
Line 2: 7 syllables
Line 3: 5 syllables

Examples

Yellow, orange, green.
Colours of the sunflowers
Painted by Van Gogh

Bright golden flowers
Standing like dolls in the fields
In yellow sunhats.

VARIATION 3

The children could design paper Japanese kites to write their poems on and display them.

FOLLOW-UP

The children could make a personal poetry anthology with examples of the different kinds of poems, haiku, lantern poems, and cinquains.

Sentence level

6.5 Shape poems

Poems which take the shape of the topic, for example, a poem about peace written in the shape of a dove.

LEVEL

1+

AGE

8+

TIME

20–25 minutes

AIMS

To write a shape poem about a chosen topic; to collect words which describe a topic; to design shapes from words.

MATERIALS

Examples of shape poems large enough for the class to see.

PREPARATION

1 Choose a theme the children have studied recently.

2 Prepare an example of a shape poem. The example below is based on a cat.

3 Draw an outline of a cat on a large sheet of paper. Make sure there are appropriate words in the word bank, or collect examples.

IN CLASS

1 Show the children your example of a shape poem.

2 Then show them the outline of the picture.

3 Elicit key words and write them in a list on the board. Ask questions like:

What is it?
What size is it?
What does it look like?
What colour is it?
What can it do?
How does it move?
What sounds can it make?
Where does it live?
What does it eat?
What does it hate?
What does it like?

4 You may get something like the following:

cat	*big*	*beautiful*
black	*white*	*jumps high*
climbs trees	*purring*	*lives in my house*
likes fish and milk	*hates dogs*	*sits in the sun*

5 Brainstorm words linked with the topic you have chosen and draft a list.

6 The children draft their poems. Monitor and check spellings.

7 Then they copy them on to a shape related to the topic. They can write round the outline of the shape or write the words inside the shape.

FOLLOW-UP

The children display their shape poems or put them in a class anthology.

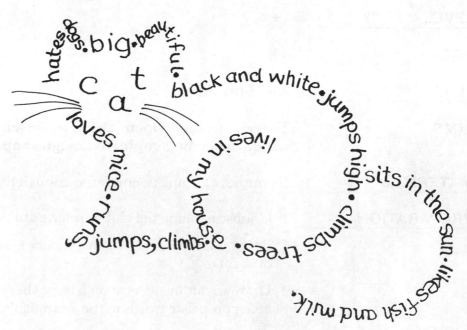

6.6 *I like/I don't like*—a class poem

LEVEL	2+
AGE	8+
TIME	**40 minutes over two lessons**
AIMS	**To use *I like/I don't like ...*; to use functions in a creative way.**
MATERIALS	Pictures of items which can generate strong likes and dislikes, for example, ice cream, cabbage, swimming, cycling, cleaning a bicycle; some card for each child or two paper plates per child, glue, scissors, stapler.
PREPARATION	

1 Make or find pictures of items that generate strong likes and dislikes in children.

2 Write or choose an example of a poem (see below).

3 Make a *Yes/No* puppet like the ones in the illustration to show the children.

4 Write an *I like/I don't like* poem to share with your children, or use one of the sample poems below.

IN CLASS

Lesson 1

1 Teach or revise *like/don't like*.

2 You could use the song 'Do you like bananas?'. Sing it to the tune of 'She'll be coming round the mountain'.

'Do you like' song

Do you like bananas?
Yes, I do.
Do you like bananas?
Yes, I do.
Do you like bananas? Do you like bananas? Do you like bananas?
Yes, I do.

Do you like cabbage?
No, I don't.
Do you like cabbage?
No, I don't.
Do you like cabbage? Do you like cabbage? Do you like cabbage?
No, I don't.

3 Demonstrate how to make a *Yes/No* puppet and give out the materials. Review the names of the items.

4 Show the pictures again, encouraging the children to show the happy or sad face of their puppet depending on what they like and don't like.

5 Make two piles of pictures: one of likes, the other of dislikes. Point to the two piles separately saying *These are the things we like. These are the things we don't like.*

6 Pick up a picture from the likes and one from the dislikes. Make a sentence, for example, *We like apples but we don't like cauliflower.*

7 Ask a child to come out and repeat this structure. Ask other children to do the same.

8 After a few examples, ask the children to work with a partner to talk about what they like and don't like. Go round and monitor.

9 Let each pair tell what they like and don't like.

10 Write the sentences on the board. Only write the same idea once.

11 Tell the children that this is the first draft of a class poem. At this stage it may look like this:

We like red apples but we don't like red peppers.
We like pizza but we don't like cabbage.
We like eating lunch but we don't like washing dishes.
We like riding bikes but we don't like cleaning them.
We like chocolate ice-cream but we don't like chocolate milk.
We like swimming in the pool but we don't like swimming in the sea.

12 Let the children write the poem on a poster.

Lesson 2

1 Ask the children to make two lists, one of things they like and another of things they don't like.

2 Remind them of the model, but using the first person: *I like … but I don't like*, for example, *I like computer games, but I don't like homework.*

3 The children create their own poems.

VARIATION

You could use *can/can't* to write different poems. This activity can operate at different levels with equal success. Younger learners can write about the things they are good at and things they do less well.

Example

> I can't ride a horse, but I can ride a bike.
> I can't speak French, but I can speak English.
> I can't drive, but I can work on the computer.
> I can't cook, but I can make good sandwiches.
> I can't make cakes, but I can eat them!

Older children can produce more reflective writing, which can help them to focus on their positive attributes.

Example

> I can't play a musical instrument, but I like music.
> I can't cook very well, but I make great pasta.
> I can't play tennis very well, but I enjoy a game with friends.
> I can't speak English very well, but I can learn some new words every day.
> I can't draw at all, but I enjoy looking at paintings.
>
> By Hiroko, aged 11

FOLLOW-UP 1

You could personalize the class poem and put it in the third person singular: *José likes …, but he doesn't like … Laura likes …, but she doesn't like …*

FOLLOW-UP 2

Make a large poster of the poem. Each child writes their line and perhaps draws a small picture to illustrate it.

6.7 Poems based on the senses

LEVEL

3+

AGE

9+

TIME

60 minutes

AIMS

Vocabulary extension and reinforcement; to reflect on feelings and the five senses; to enhance observation skills; to enhance creativity.

MATERIALS

Paper and pencils or markers, a stereo for the music, objects to challenge the five senses, for example:

smell: flower oils, things with a strong scent—sun cream or coffee, something with not such a pleasant smell like an onion or garlic

touch:	things with smooth and rough textures, for example, velvet, fake fur, satin, soft toys, a door mat, a rough stone
sight:	pictures, bright jewellery, flowers
taste:	fruit or juice, spices like cinnamon or vanilla, sweets like peppermints
hearing:	music to reflect different moods, a musical box, if possible, record some sounds like traffic noise, children playing, an aircraft, a baby crying or laughing.

PREPARATION

1 Select sample poems (see Follow-up).

2 Collect a set of objects for each of the senses.

3 Set up five centres, one for each sense.

IN CLASS

1 Create a distinctive smell in the classroom, such as lavender, before the children enter if possible (bearing in mind that preferences differ!).

2 Ask the children if they can identify the smell. Ask what it reminds them of and list the suggestions on the board. Tell them what the scent is and ask them which smells they like and which they do not like.

3 Ask which sense they used to identify the smell.

4 Ask them if they can name the other four senses. Give clues if necessary.

5 Write the names of the five senses at the top of the board and draw columns to record vocabulary.

6 Explain that they are going to use their senses to explore objects and write a poem about how smells, tastes, etc, can remind us of other things.

7 Divide the class into five groups. They visit each centre in turn and write down what each object reminds them of before moving to the next. Monitor and elicit words to help them describe their experience.

8 When everyone has visited each centre, collect the lists of words and discuss them, writing the best examples on the board in the appropriate column.

9 Explain that they are going to use their senses to write a poem. Tell them it must have five lines, one for each of the senses, about feelings like love, happiness, fun, or feelings of fear, jealousy, loneliness, or even hate if you think your children can be reflective about such feelings.

10 Show the children some examples of poems written to the following pattern: *Looks like … Sounds like … Feels like … Smells like … Tastes like …* Discuss the poems and the words used. Write some useful words on the board.

11 Give out paper and encourage the children to try out their own ideas.

12 When they have written their poems, let them read them to one another, making suggestions and editing them.

FOLLOW-UP

Let the children choose a publishing idea for their poems and add them to the class anthology, for example:

Love
Love looks like my mummy.
It sounds like my dog.
It feels like my teddy.
It smells like toast.
It tastes like chocolate ice cream.

Happiness
Happiness looks like my family.
It sounds like my dad's singing.
It feels like a warm day.
It smells like my baby sister (when she is clean!).
It tastes like pizza when I'm hungry.

By Lupita, aged 10

The following poems were written by older children and are good examples of how writing to a model can produce some fine creative writing. If the children have access to computers, they can choose a font they feel matches their poem and word-process it to put in a book or display.

Peace
Peace looks like a big park on a beautiful day.
It sounds like birds singing.
It feels like a blanket made out of towelling.
It smells like home-made cookies.
It tastes like sweet milky tea.

By Hiro, aged 12

Hate
Looks like a fire at midnight.
It sounds like silence.
It feels like boiling water.
It smells like rubber.
It tastes like a rotten lemon.

By Yuki, aged 12

COMMENTS

1 This activity works best with abstract ideas and feelings, which is why it is a good activity for older children. For younger children, you will need to choose topics you think they can cope with, for example, 'love' or 'happiness'.

2 The children can write poems individually or in pairs. It is difficult to write poems of this nature in groups.

6.8 Poems about emotions

LEVEL	2+
AGE	10+
TIME	**40–60 minutes**
AIMS	**To write poems about experiences; to express feelings.**
MATERIALS	A piece of draft paper per child, paper for the finished poems.

IN CLASS

1 Write a list of emotions across the board, for example, *happy, sad, scared, angry, surprised*. Draw a column for each one.

2 Read out the list and mimic each feeling with your facial expression, gesture and body language to indicate how that emotion makes you feel.

3 Ask the children when they have had feelings like these and what happened to make them feel that way. Record each feeling on the board with words and a smiley/sad/scared/angry/surprised face, for example, *Have you ever...*

... been lost when you were out shopping?
... fallen out with a friend?
... lost a favourite pen or toy?
... got a special present for your birthday?
... had to go to hospital?
... won an award?
... found out that someone told you a lie?
... been really scared before an exam?
*... felt really bad about the way you spoke to someone when you
      were angry or tired?*
... learnt to ride a bike?
... lost a race?

4 Give each child a piece of paper. They should choose one emotion and write it at the top of the paper. Tell them to write down what made them feel that way. When did they get those feelings? How did it make them feel inside? How did they show their feelings on the outside? What did they do?

5 The children write a sentence about each of the emotions for example, *I am happy when...* . Monitor and help with vocabulary.

6 The children write out neatly, or word-process, their finished poems.

FOLLOW-UP

You could collect the papers into a feelings box, explaining that we should take care of other people's feelings. The children can use this as a word bank (see activity 3.1).

6.9 Musical daydreaming

The children listen to music and you talk them through a possible scenario.

LEVEL	3+
AGE	10+
TIME	**30 minutes**
AIMS	**To use the rhythm of music to emphasize the importance of rhythm in writing poetry; to use music to give the writing a sense of atmosphere and pace.**
MATERIALS	A piece of music, a stereo, a script (see example below), model poems, paper, and writing materials.

PREPARATION

1 Choose a piece of music. The choice of music should affect the final outcome, so if you wish the children to write to the same rhythm, select music with a distinct rhythm they can interpret in words.

2 Prepare a script which makes use of the senses to evoke a scene.

IN CLASS

1 Tell the children to think of this activity as writing a song about the music they are going to listen to.

2 Ask the children to make themselves comfortable and close their eyes.

3 Start the music and begin to speak. Say something like:

> *Now I want you to imagine that you are dreaming.*
> *You have left school. You are in another place.*
> *Where are you?*
> *If you don't know, where do you think it is?*
> *What can you hear?*
> *What can you see?*
> *What can you smell?*
> *What can you feel?*
> *Is it spring, summer, autumn, or winter?*
> *Is it windy and warm? Or sunny and hot? Or icy and cold?*
> *Are there any buildings? What are they like?*
> *Now you are going to walk around.*
> *Are there any people?*
> *What are they like? What are they doing?*
> *Are there any children? What are they doing?*
> *Now you must come back to school.*
> *Take a good look around you before you leave.*
> *How will you get back to school?*

4 As the music ends, 'waken' the children by telling them to slowly open their eyes and sit up.

5 Give them a piece of paper and ask them to makes notes on what they have 'seen' on their journey.

6 Elicit words to describe their experiences and write useful ones on the board. Draft simple sentences with the children and then help them to put the sentences together to form poems.

Examples

A Wonderful Dream

I have a dream.
I fly into the sky.
I sing with the sun.
The song is wonderful.
I dance with the moon.
The dancing is wonderful.
I play with the stars.
The game is wonderful.
What a wonderful dream!
But it's only a dream.

By Xi Mengyuan, aged 11

Flying

I am up in the sky
I feel the sun on my back and the sky is blue.
It is warm and sunny.
I can see the streets
The people are like tiny dolls.
I see an aeroplane.
It is huge and I am small.
The people wave and I wave back at them.
I am higher than the trees.
I am higher than the highest buildings.
There are people in offices working on computers.
The children are in the playground.
They are surprised to see me come from the sky.
They are laughing and shouting round me.
They think I am from space.

By Cristina, aged 11

The Rain

The rain is coming.
The rain is cool.
The rain can get everywhere wet.
The rain makes flowers and grass grow and grow.
The raindrops fall and fall,
On my umbrella!
pitter patter, pitter patter …

By Weng Jiayin, aged 11

FOLLOW-UP   The children draw pictures of their imaginary places and display them with their poems, or put them in a class 'Imaginary journey' book.

COMMENTS   This activity could simply be responding to the sounds and rhythms of the music, or you could ask the children to make the writing actually fit the rhythm of the music. It could be used in conjunction with 5.13, 'Music as a stimulus for descriptive writing'.

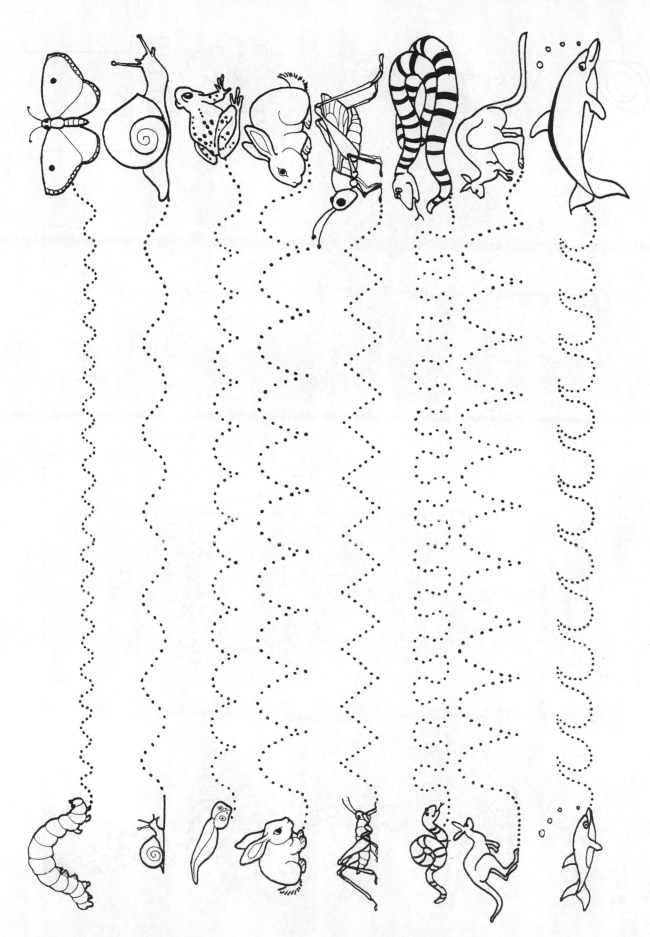

Photocopiable © Oxford University Press

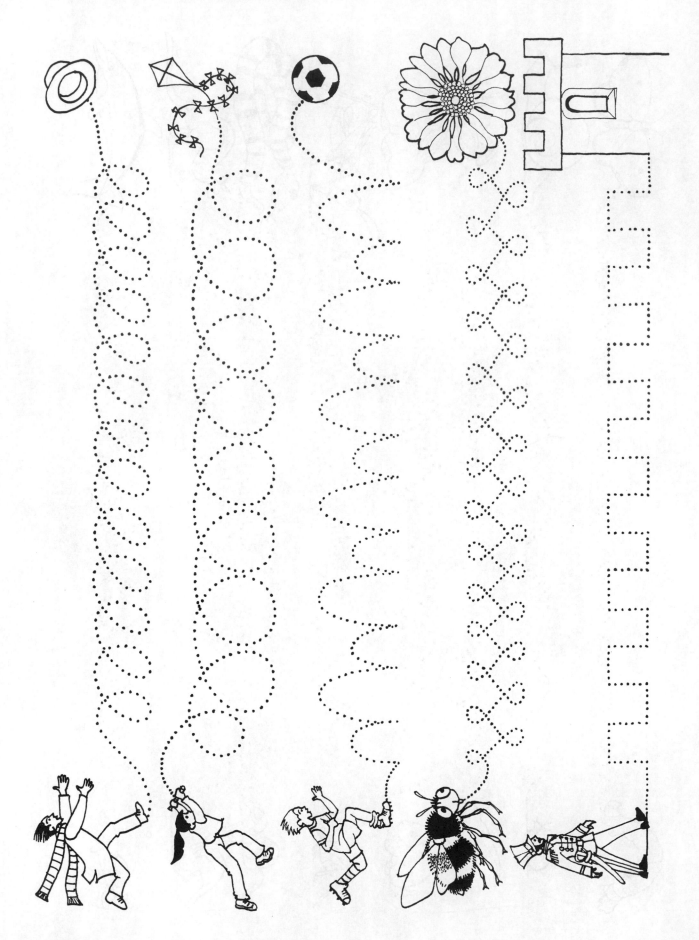

Photocopiable © Oxford University Press

Photocopiable © Oxford University Press

Photocopiable © Oxford University Press

Photocopiable © Oxford University Press

Photocopiable © Oxford University Press

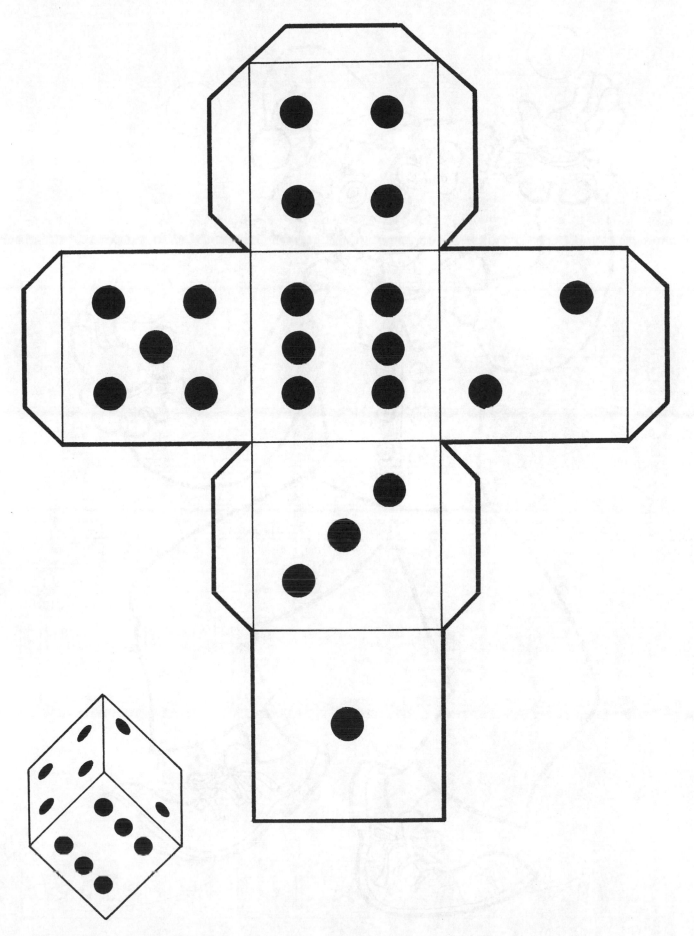

Photocopiable © Oxford University Press

Photocopiable © Oxford University Press

My name is _____ (1)

I was born in _____ (2) in _____ (3).

My father, _____ (4), is a _____ (5) and my

mother, _____ (6), is a _____ (7).

I've got _____ (8) eyes and _____ (9) hair.

I've got _____ (10) brothers and _____ (11)

sisters.

They are all very _____ (12). I've got a pet

_____ (13) called _____ (14).

Photocopiable © Oxford University Press

Find someone who _____ (name)

has an unusual hobby (what?) _____.

does their hobby every day _____

needs to do their hobby with someone else _____.

has an expensive hobby (what?) _____.

plays sport (which?) _____.

watches sport (what?) _____.

rides a horse _____.

likes making things (what?) _____.

has lessons for their hobby (what?) _____.

collects something (what?) _____.

Photocopiable © Oxford University Press

Glossary

alliteration	Two or more words repeating initial sounds close together to create a special effect, e.g. '**ch**attering **ch**ildren'. Adjective: *alliterative*.
analytic	An element of teaching *phonics* based on breaking down whole words into letters and sounds. See also *synthesis*.
articulation	Speaking clearly and distinctly.
auditory memory	The ability to remember sounds and spoken words.
balanced instruction	An approach which integrates *phonics* and *whole language*.
blend	How the constituent sounds of a word combine, e.g. *st–o–p*.
bubble wrap	Plastic sheet with air bubbles used for packing fragile articles.
cinquain	Five-line poem with 22 syllables to the verse.
cursive writing	Joined-up letters, as in adult handwriting.
decode	To *sound out* the letters in words in a *phonics* approach to reading.
digraph	Two or more letters making one sound, e.g. consonant digraphs *st*, *sh*, *th*; vowel digraphs *ar*, *aw*, *ir*.
emergent	The very early stages of reading and writing. During this stage children progress from practising the patterns of letter shapes to being introduced to the Roman alphabet and writing actual letters. At this level the children learn that each letter has a shape and a name, and makes a sound.
encode	To use knowledge of letter sounds to spell words.
flashcard	A card with a word or a picture.
genre	Type of text, e.g. stories, poems, plays, letters, reports.
grapheme	A written letter.
grapheme–phoneme correspondence	Words are composed of letters (*graphemes*) which sometimes match sounds (*phonemes*). English has less grapheme–phoneme correspondence than many languages, but there are some patterns, which form the basis of *phonics*.
guided writing	When the teacher gives individual or group support and advice about the writing task.
haiku	Japanese poetry consisting of 17 *syllables* in three lines of 5, 7, and 5 syllables.
hand–eye co-ordination/eye–hand co-ordination	The skill of guiding with the eyes the movements of the hand, as in tracing, cutting out, colouring within lines, or catching a ball.

imagery	The use of vivid descriptions and comparisons in language, which have a strong effect on imagination and feelings. See also *simile* and *metaphor*.
independent writing	After *shared* or *guided writing* the children work individually on their own writing.
initial consonant blend	English words often start with two or more consonants combined: e.g. *br-own*, *str-eet*.
lantern poetry	A poem written in a plan of five lines and counted *syllables* per line.
magic *e*	An expression used to explain to children that when a word of one syllable ends in *e*, the middle vowel becomes a long sound which usually follows the name of the letter: e.g. *cake*, *kite*, *cute*.
metaphor	A way of describing something by comparing it with something else which has the same qualities (but without using the words 'as' or 'like'). See also *simile* and *imagery*.
onset	The start of a word up to the vowel, e.g. the *r* in 'run' or *str* in 'street'.
persuasive writing	The writer holds an opinion and tries to get others to agree with him/her by using language to convince the reader to think the same way.
phoneme	The smallest functional unit of sound in a language.
phonemic awareness	The ability to isolate individual sounds and manipulate them in order to read and spell.
phonics	The teaching of letters and their corresponding sounds.
pictogram	A drawing which represents an object, an idea, or an incident.
playdough	Soft modelling dough made from flour and water. For a recipe, see the Appendix to *Art and Crafts with Children* in this series.
pre-writing	In this book, pre-writing refers to the period when children are not expected to write in English but are developing basic skills (such as *hand–eye co-ordination*) which will be needed once they reach the *emergent* and letter-writing stages.
realia	Objects used to teach meaning, e.g. real or plastic fruit.
rime	The ending of a word from the vowel onwards: e.g. *eap* in 'heap', 'cheap', 'leap'. Unlike in a *rhyme*, the letters have to be identical, but the sound does not. See also *onset*.
rhyme	Words ending in the same sound but not necessarily the same letter combination, e.g. 'beech', 'beach'.
scaffolding	A structured approach to teaching which extends children's learning by building upon what they know and designing challenging tasks to help them progress. See *Zone of Proximal Development*.

shared writing	Teacher and children create a piece of writing together, teacher demonstrating the writing process by acting as scribe.
sight-reading	Reading by recognizing whole words. See also *whole word recognition*.
sight words	Words with irregular letter patterns which can not be decoded by *sounding out*.
simile	Similes make comparisons using the words 'as' or 'like', e.g. 'her hair is as smooth as silk', whereas *metaphors* state that something *is* something else, e.g. 'love is a warm breeze'.
sounding out	Breaking down words into sections according to chunks of sound. See also *onset* and *rime*.
syllabification	Dividing a word into its constituent *syllables*.
syllable	A part of a word containing a single vowel sound. It may have one or more letters. There are three syllables in 'hos-pi-tal'. Some words have only one syllable, e.g. 'a', 'one'.
syntax	The correct order of words in a phrase, clause, or sentence.
synthesis	In *phonics*, the putting together of letters and sounds to make up a word. It also refers to teaching letter names, shapes, and sounds at the pre-writing stage. Adjective: *synthetic*.
Total Physical Response (TPR)	A teaching method which uses physical activity to make a foreign language easier to learn and remember.
visual memory	The ability to remember what one sees, i.e. the shape, colour, and size of things.
whole language	This approach involves building the children's knowledge of English through activities in which children realize that people really use English in speech, stories, and songs, not just in exercises in books or in the classroom.
whole word recognition	Identifying a word on sight from the overall shape of the word and the pattern of letters in it. See also *sight-reading*.
word families	Groups of words with the same ending sound (*rime*) but different beginnings (*onset*): for example, 'sat', 'fat', 'cat', 'mat'.
writing frames	Worksheets designed to help children to organize their writing and provide models of writing such as beginnings of sentences, key words, and, at text level, topic sentences for children to complete the paragraph.
Zone of Proximal Development	The gap between a child's current knowledge and the child's potential knowledge. It represents what the child knows now and what the teacher perceives as the child's ability to learn. The significance for the teacher lies in leading the child towards greater knowledge. See also *scaffolding*.

Acknowledgement: Some definitions are taken from the *Oxford Wordpower Dictionary*.

Further reading

Background reading

This Further reading section suggests a number of websites. The Internet is constantly changing and you may find that some websites listed here are no longer working. The book's website *www.oup.com/elt/teacher/rbt* includes links and updates.
If you find any links which are no longer working, or if you have any suggestions, please contact us via the website.

Inclusion in this list does not necessarily mean that the authors or publishers of this book endorse these sites or their content.

Asher, J. 1993. *Learning Another Language Through Actions* (4th edn). Los Gatos, CA: Sky Oaks Productions.

Askov, E. N. and **Peck, N.** 1982. 'Handwriting.' in Mitzel, H. E., Best, J. H., and Rabinowitz, W. (eds.): *Encyclopedia of Educational Research*, 5th edn. New York: Free Press.

Dahl, K. and **Scharer, P.** 2000. 'Phonics teaching and learning in whole language classrooms: New evidence from research.' *The Reading Teacher* 53: 584–94.

McLane, J. B. and **McNamee, G. D.** 1990. *Early Literacy.* Cambridge, MA: Harvard University Press.

Reyes, M. D. L. L. 1992. 'Challenging venerable assumptions.' *Harvard Educational Review* 62/4: 427–46.

Valentine, L. 2001. *Children as authors: the role of narrative writing in the EYL classroom.* Unpublished MA Dissertation. CELTE Dept., University of Warwick.

Vygotsky, L. S. 1978. *Mind in Society: The Development of Higher Psychological Processes.* Cambridge, MA: Harvard University Press.

Classroom activities

Bazo, P., Hernández, M. R., and **Peñate, M.** 1994 *Think in English A & B.* Oxford: Oxford University Press.
These two books have some very attractive word- and sentence-level activities for children who can write in their first language and have been learning English for a couple of months. Book B is a little more advanced and takes children into their second year of English.

Chaves, C., Graham, A., and **Superfine, W.** 1999. *Fun and Games in English.* Addlestone, Surrey: DELTA Publishing.
Fun activities involving reading and writing, although not all the activities develop writing.

Gray, K. (ed.) 1997/1998/1999. *Jet Primary Teachers' Resource Book 1, 2, and 3.* Addlestone, Surrey: DELTA Publishing.
Good word- and sentence-level activities.

Silver, D. M. and **Wynne, P. J.** 2002. *Adorable Wearables that Teach Early Concepts.* New York: Scholastic.

    A very useful book for teachers teaching early reading to small children. Includes hands-on alphabet learning, introducing children to basic written words through cut-outs that can be worn.

Yates, I. 1998. *Language and Literacy.* New York: Scholastic. ISBN 0-590-53756-3

    A very informative book promoting communicative development leading to re-reading/writing and early reading and writing. Many of the activities can be adapted to ESL and EFL.

http://teacher.scholastic.com/activities/bll/

    Building language for literacy (designed for native-speaker children).

Word level

Jannuzi, C. 1997. 'Key concepts in literacy: Phonics vs. Whole Language.' *Literacy Across Cultures* 1/1.

http://www2.aasa.ac.jp/~dcdycus/LAC97/phonics.htm

    A useful source which discusses the concepts of Phonics and Whole Language in EFL. *Literacy Across Cultures* is an annual publication dedicated to issues regarding the learning and teaching of reading and writing in a foreign or second language. It is published in print, online, and email versions.

Phonics

Crowther, T. G. 2004. *Up and Away.* Oxford: Oxford University Press.

    Covers initial consonant sounds, vowel sounds, blends, and digraphs but promotes a joint phonics/whole word approach to reading in English.

Eisele, C. Y., Hsieh, R., and **Sun, D.** 1997. *Mr Bug's Phonics.* Oxford: Oxford University Press.

    A course which introduces English words through amusing stories. Children practise phonics and vocabulary through songs, chants, listening activities, and writing practice.

http://www.bogglesworld.com/phonics.htm

    Phonics worksheets.

members.tripod.com/~ESL4Kids/phonics.html

    Some activities and resources designed to make both the teaching and learning of phonics more fun for you and your students.

Word games

http://curriculum.becta.org.uk/literacy/resources/website_roundup.html

    Some websites that offer word games and interactive language activities that can be used in the classroom.

Flashcards

www.enchantedlearning.com
> Provides flashcards and templates for cutting and tracing, as well as alphabet books for activities and many other useful things.

http://billybear4kids.com/
> Animal flashcards with pictures and space for writing.

http://www.abcteach.com/flashcards/adzaner.htm
> Flashcards for letter and word level, and a selection of cards in different writing styles.

Text level

Writing frames

http://www.kented.org.uk/ngfl/literacy/Writing-frames/frames1.html
> How to design writing frames and some to download.

http://www.warwick.ac.uk/staff/D.J.Wray/Ideas/frames.html
> Writing frames for older children.

Writing letters

www.talkingto.co.uk/ttws/index.asp
> The *Times Educational Supplement* has a number of sites on which children can write to famous authors, including William Shakespeare. They may ask about his life, his plays, his wife and family, the times in which he lived, fashions, the voyages of discovery around the world. The 'playwright' will answer questions within five days or alternatively he may recommend books to read or refer you to other websites. There is a database of questions already answered so children should check first whether their question has already been answered and think of another one.

Poetry

http://www.poetryzone.ndirect.co.uk/content.htm
> A gallery of children's poems you can send your children's poems to, ideas and resources for teachers, links to other sites, and suggestions for poetry books.

http://falcon.jmu.edu/~ramseyil/poechild.htm
> The Internet School Library Media Center Poetry for Children page. The ISLMC is a meta-site designed for teachers, librarians, parents, and students to preview selected curriculum-related sites.

http://www.mesalibrary.org/kids/reading_elem/poetry.aspainternet
> Multicultural poetry for children.

http://kotn.ntu.ac.uk
> The Kids on the Net site features a range of interactive activities, articles, illustrations, advice, and collaborative online writing projects which open up exciting possibilities through hypertext and multimedia.

http://www.tecnet.or.jp/~haiku/
> Children's Haiku Garden: verses and illustrations by children from around the world.

http://www.bbc.co.uk/education/listenandwrite
> Writing activities, audio poems, a gallery of children's work, and more.

Songs

Holderness, J. 2000. *Top songs.* Oxford: Oxford University Press.
> Two videos and activity books with traditional songs and ideas for using them in class. They include word-, sentence-, and text-level activities.

MacGregor, H. 1999. *Bingo Lingo.* London: A & C Black.
> A very useful song book which looks at language development, and works on the alphabet, sound patterns, and rhyming schemes.

Handwriting

http://www.preschoollearners.com
> Good quality resources and downloadable handwriting templates.

Art

http://www.enchantedlearning.com/artists/coloring
> Website with colouring pages from artists' work.

http://www.vangoghgallery.com
> Website about Van Gogh.

http://www.artcyclopedia.com
> Sources of paintings to download. Search for artists by name, for example:
> Giuseppe Arcimboldo

http://www.artcyclopedia.com/artists/arcimboldo_giuseppe.html
> Vincent Van Gogh

http://www.artcyclopedia.com/artists/van_gogh_vincent.html

http://postcards.www.media.mit.edu/PO-bin/readRack.perl?VanGogh.list/Vincent+Van+Gogh
> Electronic postcards of paintings that children can use to write messages.

Books for children

Books designed for native-speaker children

Campbell, R. 1995. *Lift-the-flap Nursery Book*. Basingstoke: Macmillan.

http://www.realbooks.co.uk/
Promotes the use of authentic children's books to motivate children to read in English, but recognizes that if the language level is too advanced, children could possibly be demotivated.

Books designed for young learners of English

All of the following have activity books and cassettes, and in some cases videos.

Briggs, R. and **Ellis, G.** 1995. *The Snowman*. Oxford: Oxford University Press.

Paul, K. and **Thomas, V.** 1995. *Winnie the Witch*. Oxford: Oxford University Press.
Winnie Flies Again (2001)
Winnie in Winter (1999)

Paul, K. and **Tzannes, R.** 1996. *Professor Puffendorf's Secret Potions*. Oxford: Oxford University Press.

Index

Other titles in the Resource Books for Teachers series

Primary Resource Books